P9-CRL-709

Reform and Transition in the Mediterranean

Series editor
Ioannis N. Grigoriadis
Bilkent University
Ankara
Turkey

"This book is a rare and significant example of comparative studies of Greece and Turkey. The two states, despite certain differences, share important characteristics in their constitutional and political development. Perhaps the most important of these common features is, as Grigoriadis convincingly argues, the majoritarian drive, with its well-known consequences such as increasing political polarization, division of the society between 'we' and 'they', 'friends and foes', the weakening of the checks and balance mechanisms, and the danger of a drift toward 'competitive authoritarianism' as described by Steven Levitsky and Lucan Way. The book supports Arend Lijphart's thesis that especially in divided societies, a 'consensus', not a 'majoritarian', model of democracy is the only workable one."
—Professor Ergun Özbudun, *İstanbul Şehir University, Turkey*

"Grigoriadis has produced a theoretically important, timely, and welcome monograph. Theoretically, it inscribes itself squarely in the distinguished tradition of Lijphart and Linz and forcefully argues in favour of 'gentler' democracies, constructed on a system of checks and balances, rooted on the rule of law, eschewing the perils of polarization associated with what Alexis de Tocqueville memorably described as the 'tyranny of the majority', and driven by a positive sum logic capable of promoting consensus and compromise in social and political discourse. In addition, its cogent criticism of the dangers of majoritarianism constitutes a most timely and convincing response to the challenges ominously brought forward by the rising tide of populism in established democracies, including the United States and Europe. Finally, the book is to be welcomed in that it succeeds in integrating two heretofore relatively undertheorized countries, Greece and Turkey, into the theoretical debates informing comparative politics."
—Professor P. Nikiforos Diamandouros, *European Ombudsman (2003–2013) and University of Athens, Greece*

The series of political and economic crises that befell many countries in the Mediterranean region starting in 2009 has raised emphatically questions of reform and transition. While the sovereign debt crisis of Southern European states and the "Arab Spring" appear *prima facie* unrelated, some common roots can be identified: low levels of social capital and trust, high incidence of corruption, and poor institutional performance. This series provides a venue for the comparative study of reform and transition in the Mediterranean within and across the political, cultural, and religious boundaries that crisscross the region. Defining the Mediterranean as the region that encompasses the countries of Southern Europe, the Levant, and North Africa, the series contributes to a better understanding of the agents and the structures that have brought reform and transition to the forefront. It invites (but is not limited to) interdisciplinary approaches that draw on political science, history, sociology, economics, anthropology, area studies, and cultural studies. Bringing together case studies of individual countries with broader comparative analyses, the series provides a home for timely and cutting-edge scholarship that addresses the structural requirements of reform and transition; the interrelations between politics, history and culture; and the strategic importance of the Mediterranean for the EU, the USA, Russia, and emerging powers.

More information about this series at
http://www.springer.com/series/14513

Ioannis N. Grigoriadis

Democratic Transition and the Rise of Populist Majoritarianism

Constitutional Reform in Greece and Turkey

Ioannis N. Grigoriadis
Department of Political Science
   and Public Administration
Bilkent University
Bilkent, Ankara
Turkey

Reform and Transition in the Mediterranean
ISBN 978-3-319-57555-1   ISBN 978-3-319-57556-8   (eBook)
DOI 10.1007/978-3-319-57556-8

Library of Congress Control Number: 2017939922

Cover illustration: Pattern adapted from an Indian cotton print produced in the 19th century

Printed on acid-free paper

This Palgrave Macmillan imprint is published by Springer Nature
The registered company is Springer International Publishing AG
The registered company address is: Gewerbestrasse 11, 6330 Cham, Switzerland

To Ishtar

FOREWORD

One of the problems with democracy is defining its boundaries. During the Cold War, we tended to assume there was a sharp contrast between the Communist states and the Western democracies, but this distinction between democracy and its opposite was never watertight, and fuzziness at the edges continues. At the end of the 1990s, the Dutch scholar Arend Lijphart, in his classic *Patterns of Democracy*, suggested that democracies could be subdivided into two categories: majoritarian and consensual. The former was close to "winner takes all" systems, such as the Westminster model, in which the winning party takes power by itself, leaving the opposition on the sidelines. By contrast, in a consensual system, such as that of Switzerland, Lijphart proposed, government power was consistently and institutionally shared between different cultural elements and opinion groups. As Ioannis N. Grigoriadis persuasively argues in this book, ultra-majoritarian systems can slip into the category of quasi-democracies, in which the locus of power is determined by the majority vote of the electorate, with the rights and interests of the minority flagrantly ignored. In short, there needs to be not only a separation of powers but also a balanced allocation of power between different institutions, to prevent the tyranny of the majority.

Greece and Turkey serve as fascinating and original examples of these processes. Although historic rivals, and occasionally enemies, the two countries are surprisingly alike in many respects, including the political. This includes a tendency towards sharp confrontation between rival political poles. In response, winners tend to suppress losers, regardless of individual rights. In the Turkish case, some of this may be explained by the Ottoman legacy. As the late Geoffrey Lewis perceptively remarked, since the 1950s Turkish politicians have tended to regard the power given to them by the electorate as analogous to that vested in the Grand Vizier, which was effectively absolute. If the Sultan was displeased with the Vizier, he could sack him (maybe execute him) but until that happened the Vizier had total authority, at least in theory. As this book persuasively argues, the widely reported trend towards authoritarianism in Turkey over the last few years is paralleled by increasingly majoritarian trends in Greece. The proposal that giving the electoral winners more power leads to more efficiency, homogeneity, and economic progress is simply untrue: Instead, experience tends to show that it exacerbates confrontational politics, contributing to clientelism and corruption, and exacerbating social divisions. In the Greek case, this book argues that polarization has made it far harder to cope with the continuing economic crisis. In Turkey, a major problem is to bridge the gap between the ethnically Turkish majority and the Kurdish minority, but majoritarianism seems likely to produce the opposite result.

This appeal for mild rather than confrontational democracy is not the only important feature of this book. Another is the simple fact that it discusses Greek and Turkish politics together, in a comparative perspective. This is a rarity: There are plenty of single-country studies of domestic and foreign policies on the one side of the Aegean or the other, but very few that look at both at once. Comparison deepens understanding of both the comparators and highlights issues which might otherwise be ignored, so that this book deserves imitation.

London, 2017

William M. Hale
Professor Emeritus, School of Oriental
and African Studies (SOAS)
University of London

PREFACE

During the completion of this study, public interest in constitutional reform has boomed. The decision of the AKP government in Turkey and the SYRIZA–ANEL coalition government in Greece to launch a constitutional amendment process has resuscitated the discussion about populist majoritarianism. While the Greek amendment process has not born any fruit by summer 2017, the Turkish voters have approved by a thin majority of 51.4 percent in the referendum of 16 April 2017 the new constitution proposed by the AKP government. The way that the public debate has unfolded has pointed at the relevance of the main findings of this study, regardless of the outcome of the amendment process. As Greek and Turkish societies remain divided on political, religious, social and other grounds and populism remains an attractive political ideology in both countries, the need to reinforce checks-and-balances mechanisms and institutions nurturing social trust remains imperative.

Princeton, NJ   Ioannis N. Grigoriadis

ACKNOWLEDGEMENTS

An earlier, shorter version of this study won a prize at the 2013 Sabancı University Annual Research Award competition. The author would like to thank Onur Kutlu, Akis Sakellariou and Çağkan Korur for their ample research assistance.

I would also like to thank my friends and colleagues Iosif Kovras and Neophytos Loizides whose article on majoritarianism and the Greek economic crisis helped me develop my original argument.

Thanks are also due to the anonymous reviewers of the *Journal of Modern Greek Studies* for the useful feedback they gave to an early draft.

Finally, I would like to recognize the support of Stiftung Mercator, the German Institute for International and Security Affairs (Stiftung Wissenschaft und Politik-SWP) and the Seeger Center for Hellenic Studies, Princeton University. The SWP and the Seeger Center hosted me as IPC-Stiftung Mercator Senior Research Fellow and Stanley J. Seeger Visiting Research Fellow respectively in the academic year 2016–2017, when this work was completed.

CONTENTS

ABOUT THE AUTHOR

Dr. Ioannis N. Grigoriadis is Associate Professor and Jean Monnet Chair at the Department of Political Science and Public Administration, Bilkent University. In the academic year 2016–2017, he was an IPC-Stiftung Mercator Senior Research Fellow at the German Institute for International and Security Affairs (*Stiftung Wissenschaft und Politik-SWP*) in Berlin and a Stanley J. Seeger Research Fellow at Princeton University. Between 2004 and 2009, he taught at Sabancı University, Işık University and the University of Athens. His research interests include European, Turkish politics, nationalism and democratization. His recent publications include two books, *Instilling Religion in Greek and Turkish Nationalism: A "Sacred Synthesis"* (London and New York: Palgrave Macmillan, 2012) and *Trials of Europeanization: Turkish Political Culture and the European Union*, (London and New York: Palgrave Macmillan, 2009). He has also authored several journal articles. These include "Energy Discoveries in the Eastern Mediterranean: Conflict or Cooperation?", *Middle East Policy*, Vol. XXI, No. 3, Fall 2014, pp. 124–133, "Reform Paradoxes: Academic Freedom and Governance in Greek and Turkish Higher Education", *Southeast European and Black Sea Studies*, Vol. 12, No. 1, March 2012, pp. 135–152 (with Antonis Kamaras), "Friends No More?: The Rise of Anti-American Nationalism in Turkey", *Middle East Journal*, Vol. 64, No. 1, Winter 2010, pp. 51–66, "Islam and Democratization in Turkey: Secularism and Trust in a Divided Society", *Democratization*, Vol. 16,

No. 6, December 2009, pp. 1194–1213 and "On the Europeanization of Minority Rights Protection: Comparing the Cases of Greece and Turkey", *Mediterranean Politics*, Vol. 13, No. 1, March 2008, pp. 23–41.

ABBREVIATIONS

AKP	Adalet ve Kalkınma Partisi-Justice and Development Party
ANAP	Anavatan Partisi-Motherland Party
ANEL	Anexartitoi Ellines-Independent Greeks
CHP	Cumhuriyet Halk Partisi-Republican People's Party
DP	Demokrat Parti-Democrat Party
DSP	Demokratik Sol Partisi-Democratic Left Party
ECB	European Central Bank
EEC	European Economic Community
EU	European Union
HDP	Halkların Demokratik Partisi-Peoples' Democratic Party
HSYK	Hâkimler ve Savcılar Yüksek Kurulu-Supreme Board of Judges and Prosecutors
IMF	International Monetary Fund
KKE	Kommounistiko Komma Ellados-Communist Party of Greece
MGK	Milli Güvenlik Kurulu-National Security Council
MHP	Milliyetçi Hareket Partisi-Nationalist Action Party
NATO	North Atlantic Treaty Organization
ND	Nea Dimokratia-New Democracy
PASOK	Panellinio Sosialistiko Kinima-Panhellenic Socialist Movement
RP	Refah Partisi-Welfare Party
SYRIZA	Synaspismos Rizospastikis Aristeras-Coalition of Radical Left

LIST OF FIGURES

ABSTRACT

This study explores in a comparative perspective the impact of populist majoritarianism on Greek and Turkish constitutional reform. While majoritarianism features as an element of numerous democratic regimes and often celebrated as a manifestation of popular sovereignty, it can be championed by populist leaders and foment polarization, undermine institutional performance and even entangle the process of democratic consolidation. It may contribute to a confrontational and inefficient democratic regime in cases of transition states where levels of social capital are low. The study of the Greek transition to democracy shows us that the dominance of populist majoritarianism can stifle pluralism, weaken checks-and-balances mechanisms, contribute to the consolidation of clientelism, foster corruption, deepen social divisions and weaken institutional performance. These have been among the key underlying factors for the profound political, economic and social crisis that has befallen Greece since 2009. The Greek experience can be highly instructive about the inherent risks of a majoritarian takeover in Turkey. A populist majoritarian shift in Turkish politics through constitutional reform is likely to have similar deleterious effects regarding social cohesion, institutional performance and corruption. Building up a "mild democracy" requires maturity of institutions, an efficient system of checks-and-balances and implementation control mechanisms. This could lead to a shift from a "zero-sum" to a "positive sum game" approach in the resolution of domestic political disputes. Developing consensus and trust in societies torn by ethnic, religious and ideological divides is not a luxury but a permissive condition for democratic consolidation, institutional performance, social cohesion and economic prosperity. Recent developments in Turkey seem to corroborate concerns that a majoritarian takeover may occur at the peril of institutional performance and democratic consolidation.

CHAPTER 1

Introduction

Abstract This chapter introduces the terms "majoritarianism" and "populism", the distinction between majoritarian and consensus democracies, and goes over the respective criteria, according to the literature on democracy. While majoritarianism refers to the rule of the majority without any consideration of the views or the rights of the minority, consensus democracy refers to the rule of as big a majority as possible. It then justifies the choice of Greece and Turkey as cases where majoritarianism has witnessed a rise in the context of democratic transition.

Keywords Majoritarianism · Populism · Consensus
Democratization · Greece · Turkey · Democracy

MAJORITARIAN VERSUS CONSENSUS DEMOCRACIES

The debate about the ideal type of a democratic regime is a long and heated one and pervades the history of political science. Fine-tuning a balance between the "rule of the many" and the "rights of the few" has been a constant preoccupation of democratic political thinkers and practitioners. From the absolute, unconditional rule (or tyranny) of majority to the exhaustive deliberations until even the smallest citizen groups are convinced about the wisdom of a political decision, different solutions have been suggested. One of the key ways of crystallizing this debate has been through the juxtaposition of majoritarian and

© The Author(s) 2018
I.N. Grigoriadis, *Democratic Transition and the Rise of Populist Majoritarianism*, Reform and Transition in the Mediterranean,
DOI 10.1007/978-3-319-57556-8_1

consensus democracy.[1] Between these two Weberian ideal types, all democratic regimes can be placed. Lijphart, arguably the scholar that has contributed the most to this important debate, has identified nine criteria for the definition of a consensus vs. a majoritarian democratic regime, as follows:

> (1) broad coalition cabinets instead of one-party bare-majority cabinets; (2) a balanced power relationship between the cabinet and the legislature instead of cabinet predominance; (3) a bicameral legislature, particularly one in which the two chambers have roughly equal powers and are differently constituted, instead of unicameralism; (4) a federal and decentralized structure instead of unitary and centralized government; (5) a "rigid" constitution that can only be amended by extraordinary majorities, instead of a "flexible" written or unwritten constitution; (6) judicial review of the constitutionality of legislation; (7) a multiparty instead of a two-party system; (8) a multidimensional party system, in which the parties differ from each other on one or more issue dimensions in addition to socioeconomic issues, for instance, along religious, cultural-ethnic, urban-rural, or foreign policy dimensions; and (9) elections by proportional representation instead of by plurality.[2]

As consecutive waves of democratization in the twentieth century led to an ever-growing number of states that could be qualified as democratic, the debate between proponents of majoritarian and consensus democracies flourished.[3] The virtues and vices of majoritarianism have been explored in different regional and temporal contexts,[4] by means of comparing presidential, semi-presidential and parliamentary regimes.[5] Several scholars have identified the prevalence of majoritarian elements as an indication of institutional underperformance, particularly in the context of states that had only recently gone through a democratic transition.[6] Linz pointed the dangers of polarization in a fashion that points not only to presidential but also to all majoritarian regimes, as follows:

> Winners and losers are sharply defined for the entire period of the presidential mandate. There is no hope for shifts in alliances, expansion of the government's base of support through national-unity or emergency grand coalitions, new elections in response to major new events, and so on. Instead, the losers must wait at least four or five years without any access to executive power and patronage. The zero-sum game in presidential regimes raises the stakes of presidential elections and inevitably exacerbates their attendant tension and polarization.[7]

In this light, the performance of democratic regimes in Latin America and Southern Europe has been evaluated and contrasted with the majoritarian features of the US[8] and French democratic regimes, as well as the consensus features of Germany and Nordic states. Southern Europe[9] and Latin America[10] have attracted considerable attention, given their recent transition to democracy and the challenges their democratic regimes faced in establishing sound and resilient institutions.[11] Merkel's concept of embedded democracy acquired high relevance in this context, pointing not only at the diversity of democratic institutions, but also at the challenges faced by democracy in different institutional and cultural contexts.[12]

DEFINING POPULISM

A discussion about majoritarianism in the Greek and Turkish context would not be complete without addressing the question of populism, a topic that has recently acquired increased interest.[13] A subject of conceptual confusion, populism has been praised by some as "a path to true democracy" and despised by others as "proto-fascism". While one could not object to some key populist demands such as the involvement of the people into the political process or the "government of the people, by the people, for the people" in the way Abraham Lincoln famously put in his 1863 Gettysburg Address, it is important to remember that adherence to populism usually coincides with illiberal leanings, intolerance towards dissidence and diversity. In fact, opposition to liberal democracy has proven to be one of the most enduring features of populists across the globe. This study follows the definition of Mudde and Kaltwasser according to which, populism is

> a thin-centred ideology that considers society to be ultimately separated into two homogeneous and antagonistic camps, "the pure people" versus "the corrupt elite" and which argues that politics should be an expression of the *volonté générale* (general will) of the people.[14]

One needs to clarify that inviting the people into the political debate is in itself anything but negative. The rise of populism often emerges as a healthy reminder about the need to engage the public in the political process, which often becomes too arcane and seemingly irrelevant to peoples' lives. On the other hand, the appeal to the people often moves further to identify as key political demand the emancipation of a "pure" and "infallible" people which suffers under a "corrupt" and "illegitimate" elite. In that context, appealing to the *volonté générale* of the people in a Rousseauian sense as the sole yardstick of what is politically expedient and useful paves the way for the adoption of majoritarian views and growing intolerance, marginalization or even silencing of minority voices within the political arena.

When populists come to power, then a paradox is due to emerge, since the fiercest critics of the elites become elites themselves. Nevertheless, populist leaders have repeatedly claimed—and often with remarkable persuasiveness—that "corrupt" elites maintained their influence even after their rise to government and thus continued to limit the exercise of democratic popular sovereignty. Making use of that pretext, populist governance is characterized according to Müller by three features:

> attempts to hijack the state apparatus, corruption and "mass clientelism" (trading material benefits or bureaucratic favours for political support by citizens who become the populists' "clients") and efforts systematically to suppress civil society.[15]

Given the thin conceptual content of populism, it can borrow symbolic resources or be fully integrated with other mainstream ideologies, left- or right-wing: Nationalism, socialism and conservatism, religious or not, can imbue populism with features that produce a more resilient and context-specific political ideology. As it will become clear later, on account of their divergent historical experiences, it is no surprise that left-wing nationalist populism would thrive in Greece and right-wing nationalist populism in Turkey. Both of them engaged in constitutional reform projects aiming to promote a majoritarian vision of democracy, mirroring their claim of being the sole representative and defender of the people against its enemies, as well as their disrespect for social pluralism and minority views. The concomitant attempts to control the state apparatus through the establishment of clientelistic networks could not put the integrity of state institutions and government performance under severe pressure.

CASE SELECTION-THESIS

Why choose Greece and Turkey to study the effects of populist majoritarianism through the study of their constitutions? The selection of Greece and Turkey as cases for this comparative study is due to the common features of their historic experience[16] and its relevance for a number of other countries in the European periphery.

At least since 1974 Greece and Turkey have followed divergent paths as far as their dominant political discourse is concerned. Following the collapse of the 1967–1974 military regime, Greece has been mainly governed by populist parties on the left of the political spectrum. In Turkey the hegemon is different: At least since the 1980–1983 military regime, the Turkish right has enjoyed long government rule and ideological domination. While hegemonic parties are different, some of the key terms of their political and ideological vocabulary are not. The political hegemony of the left represented by PASOK and SYRIZA (its post-crisis successor) in post-1981 Greece and of the conservative right represented by the ANAP and DYP in the 1980s and the 1990s and by the AKP in post-2002 Turkey have been contingent upon the populist instrumentalization of prior social divides, dating to the 1946–1949 civil war and its aftermath in Greece and the Atatürk reform and its consequences in Turkey. In other words, precedent social divisions emerged as a useful opportunity structure[17] for the Greek left and the Turkish right for the consolidation of their hegemonic position through the promotion of populist majoritarianism.

A rhetoric of exceptionalism, victimhood, a Manichean division of the society between the good "betrayed" people and the bad "treacherous" elites fitted very well the interests of both hegemonic political movements. Consolidating the ideological divisions of both societies gave these parties the chance to cement their flanks, prevent electoral losses due to poor government performance and preclude a discussion about their own political shortcomings. Election or referendum campaigns were framed along binary identity and normative lines, "us" versus "them." Under these conditions, it was reasonable to underscore a majoritarian understanding of democracy whereby institutions become the instruments for the realization of *volonté générale* against the elites. In these views, "real democracy" came to Greece and Turkey in 1981 and 2002, respectively.

Moreover, both countries have had a strong tradition of military tutelage over politics in the twentieth century and struggled through their transition to democracy. While the constitutional authors of both countries were aware of the perils of power concentration in the hands of the executive, they attempted to create institutional barriers against it. As Greece moved faster in the direction of democratic consolidation, its regime also faced an earlier majoritarian challenge. The experience of Greece and the debate that has been recently introduced in both Greece and Turkey regarding an amendment of the constitution can be highly instructive. Transition states in Eastern Europe and in the Mediterranean may face similar challenges in the near future. The case of Hungary under the rule of Viktor Orban is one example.

This study aims to promote and contextualize the debate introduced by the seminal studies of Lijphart on the correlation between democracy type and government performance. Emerging from military authoritarianism countries like Greece, Spain and Portugal set the foundations for the consolidation of their respective democratic regimes in the 1970s. Membership of the European Economic Community (EEC) became one of the most important anchors and was perceived as reward for this transition. The calibration of institutional checks and balances has been one of the most sensitive questions in that process. This study aims to investigate how populist majoritarianism rose to shape Greek and Turkish[18] democratic transition and dominate constitutional debates.[19] While Greece and Turkey had experienced democratic consolidation with a time lag of approximately three decades, both shared some common features. Having emerged from authoritarian military regimes that had overturned post-Second World War procedural democracies, constitutional deliberations focused on how to consolidate popular sovereignty and better protect nascent democratic institutions against the power of influential but not democratically legitimized bureaucratic veto-holders. State elites were seen not as partners in that process, but as enemies and vestiges of a semi-authoritarian past that had to be obliterated. Populist parties led this process in both states; their success underscored the perpetuation of social and political divisions within the Greek and Turkish society.

Why study majoritarianism through constitutions? Constitutions are the cornerstones of political regimes, and their study is essential both in order to understand their main features, as well as identify further areas of reform. Through the study of the constitutional history of Greece and

Turkey, it becomes easier to study the rise of populist majoritarianism in the context of democratic consolidation. Exploring key fault lines that have contributed to the definition of Greek and Turkish constitutional politics is of paramount significance, as it helps better understand the existing institutional shortcomings and suggest solutions for improving the quality of democratic regimes.

This study argues that, while majoritarianism is not intrinsically linked with a presidential or a parliamentary regime, populism-driven constitutional reform reinforcing majoritarian features is likely to lead to institutional underperformance in either of the two.[20] It also correlates with a confrontational and inefficient democratic regime in cases of transition states where polarization along ethnic and social lines remains high, levels of social capital are low and poor institutional performance means that the power of the executive can remain virtually unchecked. The study of the rise of populist majoritarianism in Greece and Turkey through constitutional reform shows how social divisions can be politically manipulated and pluralism can be stifled. Rising majoritarianism could then contribute to the subordination of state bureaucracy to party clientelistic networks, reduce institutional performance, deepen social divisions, foster corruption and in the end impede democratic consolidation. The dilution of existing checks and balances, the fragmentation of society and the disintegration of state bureaucracy have been among the key underlying factors for the profound economic and social crisis that has befallen Greece since 2009, in particular about its unrivalled resilience. Unlike other EU states that faced a severe economic crisis following the global financial crisis of 2008 but were able to record a swift recovery, Greece has been caught in a vicious circle of reform failure and depression. The Greek experience can be highly instructive about the inherent risks of this process in Turkey. As populism-driven majoritarianism has been one of the main contributing factors to the current Greek economic and political crisis, the prospects of a decisive shift toward populist majoritarianism in Turkey would not bode well for the quality of the Turkish democratic regime, especially given Turkey's deep social divisions. Turkey's democratic transition process is likely to face a critical quality check, if democratic checks-and-balances mechanisms are corroded through a constitutional reform introducing a strong presidential system. This study concurs with one of the conclusions of Lijphart that a participant political culture functions as permissive condition for a smooth transition towards consensus democracy.[21]

Chapters 2 and 3 focus on the constitutional politics and democratic transition of Greece and Turkey, respectively, while Chaps. 4 and 5 explore the rise of populist majoritarianism in both states through the politics of constitutional reform. Chapter 6 discusses majoritarianism and state performance in Greece and Turkey, while Chap. 7 concludes by revisiting the main thesis of this study.

NOTES

1. Arend Lijphart, *Thinking About Democracy: Power Sharing and Majority Rule in Theory and Practice* (London & New York: Routledge 2007), pp. 215–216 and 2012).

2. Arend Lijphart, *Patterns of Democracy: Government Forms and Performance in Thirty-Six Countries* (New Haven, CT: Yale University Press, 1999), pp. 34–47. For more insights into the topic, see also Arend Lijphart, *Democracies: Patterns of Majoritarian and Consensus Government in Twenty-One Countries* (New Haven CT: Yale University Press, 1984), pp. 1–36 cited by Arend Lijphart, "Majoritarian Versus Consensual Democracy" in Bernard E. Brown, ed., *Comparative Politics: Notes and Readings* (New York: Harcourt College, 1991b), p. 176, Jon Elster, "On Majoritarianism and Rights", *E. Eur. Const. Rev.*, Vol. 19, no. 1 (1992). On the question of classification, see also Jeffrey J. Anderson, "Europeanization and the Transformation of the Democratic Polity, 1945–2000", *JCMS: Journal of Common Market Studies*, Vol. 40, no. 5 (2002), pp. 800–815.

3. See, for example, Juan J. Linz, "Presidential or Parliamentary Democracy: Does It Make a Difference?" in Juan J. Linz and Arturo Valenzuela, eds., *The Crisis of Presidential Democracy: The Latin American Evidence* (Baltimore: Johns Hopkins University Press, 1994), Arend Lijphart, "Constitutional Choices for New Democracies", *Journal of Democracy*, Vol. 2, no. 1 (1991a) and Arend Lijphart, "Introduction" in Arend Lijphart, ed., *Parliamentary Versus Presidential Government* (Oxford: Oxford University Press, 1992).

4. See, for example, Arend Lijphart, *Patterns of Democracy: Government Forms and Performance in 36 Countries* (New Haven, CT: Yale University Press, 1999).

5. On this, see Alfred Stepan and Cindy Skach, "Constitutional Frameworks and Democratic Consolidation: Parliamentarianism Versus Presidentialism", *World Politics*, Vol. 46, no. 01 (1993), Alan Siaroff, "Comparative Presidencies: The Inadequacy of the Presidential, Semi-Presidential and Parliamentary Distinction", *European Journal of Political*

Research, Vol. 42, no. 3 (2003), Matthew S. Shugart, "Of Presidents and Parliaments", *East European Constitutional Review*, Vol. 2, no. 1 (1993) and José Antônio Cheibub, *Presidentialism, Parliamentarism, and Democracy* (New York, NY: Cambridge University Press, 2007). For a critique of parliamentary democracy, see Kaare Strøm, "Parliamentary Democracy: Promise and Problems" in Wolfgang C. Müller, Bergman Torbjörn and Kaare Strøm, eds., *Delegation and Accountability in Parliamentary Democracies* (Oxford: Oxford University Press, 2006).

6. On this, see Scott Mainwaring, "Presidentialism, Multipartism, and Democracy: The Difficult Combination", *Comparative Political Studies*, Vol. 26, no. 2 (1993), Juan J Linz and Arturo Valenzuela, *The Failure of Presidential Democracy* (Baltimore: Johns Hopkins University Press, 1994), Scott Mainwaring and Matthew S Shugart, "Juan Linz, Presidentialism, and Democracy: A Critical Appraisal", *Comparative Politics* (1997).

7. Juan J. Linz, "The Perils of Presidentialism", *Journal of Democracy*, Vol. 1, no. 1 (1990), p. 56.

8. On this, see Bruce A. Ackerman, *The Failure of the Founding Fathers: Jefferson, Marshall, and the Rise of Presidential Democracy* (Cambridge, MA: Belknap Press of Harvard University Press, 2005).

9. On the relationship between democratization in Southern Europe and presidentialism, see Arend Lijphart, "The Southern European Examples of Democratization: Six Lessons for Latin America", *Government and Opposition*, Vol. 25, no. 1 (1990) and Arend Lijphart et al., "A Mediterranean Model of Democracy? The Southern European Democracies in Comparative Perspective", *West European Politics*, Vol. 11, no. 1 (1988).

10. For a dissenting view in favour of presidentialism, see Julio Faundez, "In Defense of Presidentialism: The Case of Chile, 1932–1970" in Scott Mainwaring and Matthew S. Shugart, eds., *Presidentialism and Democracy in Latin America* (Cambridge: Cambridge University Press, 1997).

11. On a classic study, see Nicos P. Mouzelis, *Politics in the Semi-Periphery: Early Parliamentarism and Late Industrialization in the Balkans and Latin America* (New York: St. Martin's Press, 1986).

12. Wolfgang Merkel, "Embedded and Defective Democracies", *Democratization*, Vol. 11, no. 5 (2004), pp. 44–48. Also see Cengiz Erisen and Paul Kubicek, "Conceptualizing Democratic Consolidation in Turkey" in Cengiz Erisen and Paul Kubicek, eds., *Democratic Consolidation in Turkey: Micro and Macro Challenges* (Oxford & New York: Routledge, 2016a).

13. The affirmative result of the "Brexit" referendum on 23 June 2016 and the November 2016 election of Donald Trump as president of the United States were two of the most spectacular successes of populist politicians and politics in the developed world. See Senem Aydın-Düzgit and E. Fuat Keyman, *The Trump Presidency and the Rise of Populism in the Global Context* (Istanbul: Istanbul Policy Center (IPC), 2017).

14. Cas Mudde and Cristobal Rovira Kaltwasser, *Populism: A Very Short Introduction* (Oxford & New York: Oxford University Press, 2017), pp. 5–6.

15. Jan-Werner Muller, *What Is Populism?* (Philadelphia: University of Pennsylvania Press 2016), p. 4.

16. On this, also see Thanos Veremis, *Greeks and Turks in War and Peace* (Athens: Athens News 2007).

17. On the term "opportunity structure", see Hanspeter Kriesi, "The Political Opportunity Structure of New Social Movements: Its Impact on Their Mobilization" in J. Craig Jenkins and Bert Klandermans, eds., *The Politics of Social Protest: Comparative Perspectives on States and Social Movements,* 1995), pp. 167–170.

18. On Turkey's experience of majoritarianism, see Cengiz Erisen and Paul Kubicek, eds., *Democratic Consolidation in Turkey: Micro and Macro Challenges* (Oxford & New York: Routledge, 2016b).

19. On the question of the durability of constitutions and their amendments, see Zachary Elkins, Tom Ginsburg and James Melton, *The Endurance of National Constitutions* (Cambridge; New York: Cambridge University Press, 2009).

20. On the role of veto players in presidential and parliamentary systems, see George Tsebelis, "Decision Making in Political Systems: Veto Players in Presidentialism, Parliamentarism, Multicameralism and Multipartyism", *British Journal of Political Science,* Vol. 25, no. 3 (1996), pp. 318–322.

21. Lijphart, *Patterns of Democracy: Government Forms and Performance in 36 Countries,* p. 306.

References

Bruce A. Ackerman, *The Failure of the Founding Fathers: Jefferson, Marshall, and the Rise of Presidential Democracy* (Cambridge, MA: Belknap Press of Harvard University Press, 2005).

Jeffrey J. Anderson, "Europeanization and the Transformation of the Democratic Polity, 1945–2000", *JCMS: Journal of Common Market Studies,* Vol. 40, no. 5 (2002), pp. 793–822.

Senem Aydın-Düzgit and E. Fuat Keyman, *The Trump Presidency and the Rise of Populism in the Global Context* (Istanbul: Istanbul Policy Center (IPC), 2017).

José Antônio Cheibub, *Presidentialism, Parliamentarism, and Democracy* (New York, NY: Cambridge University Press, 2007).

Zachary Elkins, Tom Ginsburg and James Melton, *The Endurance of National Constitutions* (Cambridge; New York: Cambridge University Press, 2009).

Jon Elster, "On Majoritarianism and Rights", *E. Eur. Const. Rev.*, Vol. 19, no. 1 (1992), pp. 19–24.

Cengiz Erisen and Paul Kubicek, "Conceptualizing Democratic Consolidation in Turkey" in Cengiz Erisen and Paul Kubicek, eds., *Democratic Consolidation in Turkey: Micro and Macro Challenges* (Oxford & New York: Routledge, 2016a), pp. 1–18.

Cengiz Erisen and Paul Kubicek, eds., *Democratic Consolidation in Turkey: Micro and Macro Challenges* (Oxford & New York: Routledge, 2016b).

Julio Faundez, "In Defense of Presidentialism: The Case of Chile, 1932–1970" in Scott Mainwaring and Matthew S. Shugart, eds., *Presidentialism and Democracy in Latin America* (Cambridge: Cambridge University Press, 1997).

Hanspeter Kriesi, "The Political Opportunity Structure of New Social Movements: Its Impact on Their Mobilization" in J. Craig Jenkins and Bert Klandermans, eds., *The Politics of Social Protest: Comparative Perspectives on States and Social Movements*, 1995, pp. 167–98.

Arend Lijphart, *Democracies: Patterns of Majoritarian and Consensus Government in Twenty-One Countries* (New Haven, CT: Yale University Press, 1984).

Arend Lijphart, Thomas C. Bruneau, P. Nikiforos Diamandouros and Richard Gunther, "A Mediterranean Model of Democracy? The Southern European Democracies in Comparative Perspective", *West European Politics*, Vol. 11, no. 1 (1988), pp. 7–25.

Arend Lijphart, "The Southern European Examples of Democratization: Six Lessons for Latin America", *Government and Opposition*, Vol. 25, no. 1 (1990), pp. 68–84.

Arend Lijphart, "Constitutional Choices for New Democracies", *Journal of Democracy*, Vol. 2, no. 1 (1991a), pp. 73–84.

Arend Lijphart, "Majoritarian Versus Consensual Democracy" in Bernard E. Brown, ed., *Comparative Politics: Notes and Readings* (New York: Harcourt College, 1991b), pp. 175–84.

Arend Lijphart, "Introduction" in Arend Lijphart, ed., *Parliamentary Versus Presidential Government* (Oxford: Oxford University Press, 1992), pp. 1–30.

Arend Lijphart, *Patterns of Democracy: Government Forms and Performance in Thirty-Six Countries* (New Haven, CT: Yale University Press, 1999).

Arend Lijphart, *Thinking About Democracy: Power Sharing and Majority Rule in Theory and Practice* (London & New York: Routledge, 2007).

Arend Lijphart, *Patterns of Democracy: Government Forms and Performance in Thirty-Six Countries* (New Haven, CT: Yale University Press, 2012).

Juan J. Linz, "The Perils of Presidentialism", *Journal of Democracy*, Vol. 1, no. 1 (1990), pp. 51–69.

Juan J. Linz and Arturo Valenzuela, *The Failure of Presidential Democracy* (Baltimore: Johns Hopkins University Press, 1994).

Juan J. Linz, "Presidential or Parliamentary Democracy: Does It Make a Difference?" in Juan J. Linz and Arturo Valenzuela, eds., *The Crisis of Presidential Democracy: The Latin American Evidence* (Baltimore: Johns Hopkins University Press, 1994), pp. 3–87.

Scott Mainwaring, "Presidentialism, Multipartism, and Democracy: The Difficult Combination", *Comparative Political Studies*, Vol. 26, no. 2 (1993), pp. 198–228.

Scott Mainwaring and Matthew S Shugart, "Juan Linz, Presidentialism, and Democracy: A Critical Appraisal", *Comparative Politics* (1997), pp. 449–71.

Wolfgang Merkel, "Embedded and Defective Democracies", *Democratization*, Vol. 11, no. 5 (2004), pp. 33–58.

Nicos P. Mouzelis, *Politics in the Semi-Periphery: Early Parliamentarism and Late Industrialization in the Balkans and Latin America* (New York: St. Martin's Press, 1986).

Cas Mudde and Cristobal Rovira Kaltwasser, *Populism: A Very Short Introduction* (Oxford & New York: Oxford University Press, 2017).

Jan-Werner Muller, *What Is Populism?* (Philadelphia: University of Pennsylvania Press, 2016).

Matthew S. Shugart, "Of Presidents and Parliaments", *East European Constitutional Review*, Vol. 2, no. 1 (1993), pp. 30–32.

Alan Siaroff, "Comparative Presidencies: The Inadequacy of the Presidential, Semi-Presidential and Parliamentary Distinction", *European Journal of Political Research*, Vol. 42, no. 3 (2003), pp. 287–312.

Alfred Stepan and Cindy Skach, "Constitutional Frameworks and Democratic Consolidation: Parliamentarianism Versus Presidentialism", *World Politics*, Vol. 46, no. 1 (1993), pp. 1–22.

Kaare Strøm, "Parliamentary Democracy: Promise and Problems" in Wolfgang C. Müller, Bergman Torbjörn and Kaare Strøm, eds., *Delegation and Accountability in Parliamentary Democracies* (Oxford: Oxford University Press, 2006), pp. 55–108.

George Tsebelis, "Decision Making in Political Systems: Veto Players in Presidentialism, Parliamentarism, Multicameralism and Multipartyism", *British Journal of Political Science*, Vol. 25, no. 3 (1996), pp. 289–325.

Thanos Veremis, *Greeks and Turks in War and Peace* (Athens: Athens News, 2007).

CHAPTER 2

Democratic Transition in Greece

Abstract Since its independence in 1830, Greece's path towards democratic consolidation has been non-linear and uneven. Following the collapse of the 1967–1974 military regime, a new democratic constitution was promulgated in 1975. Parliamentary debates on the constitutional draft reflected different approaches on the question of majoritarianism between the parties that would dominate Greek politics, New Democracy and PASOK. Despite its radical rhetoric, the rise of PASOK to power in 1981 did not question Greece's membership of Western organizations and NATO and did not affect the harmonious cooperation between the president and the prime minister.

Keywords PASOK · New democracy · Karamanlis · Papandreou
Venizelos · Civil war

INTRODUCTION

Greece comprises a rather interesting case in the study of democratic transitions, being the single case of involvement in all three forward and in both reverse democratization waves.[1] Inevitably, Greece's constitutional history has been a reflection of the country's uneven and non-linear path towards democratic consolidation.

Since the fall of the 1967–1974 military regime, Greece has gone through the longest period of uninterrupted democratic rule in its

© The Author(s) 2018   13
I.N. Grigoriadis, *Democratic Transition and the Rise of Populist Majoritarianism*, Reform and Transition in the Mediterranean,
DOI 10.1007/978-3-319-57556-8_2

history. Following the promulgation of a republican constitution in 1975, its membership of the European Economic Community (EEC) in 1981 proved to be one of the crucial anchors of Greece's democratic regime. One major (1986) and two minor constitutional amendments (2001 and 2008) have led to heated debates about majoritarianism but have not shaken the foundations of the post-1974 order. Only the economic crisis that has hit the country since 2009 has questioned the resilience of Greek democratic institutions and contributed to discussions about the root causes of the crisis and the role of the constitution.

CONSTITUTIONAL HISTORY

Even before the outbreak of the Greek War of Independence in 1821, there had been a vibrant debate about the republican nature of the new regime and the protection of fundamental rights and freedoms through the introduction of a constitution. While there were three revolutionary constitutions that attempted to establish a liberal democratic blueprint for the emerging Greek nation-state, these were eventually neglected, as the independence of Greece was conditioned upon the consent of European autocracies. Hence, according to the Protocol of London of 2 February 1830 and the Treaty of Constantinople of 9 July 1832, the independent Kingdom of Greece became an absolute monarchy. State building under the Triumvirate introduced to the underage King Otto von Wittelsbach followed the autocratic blueprint of post-Napoleonic Europe. Only after the 3 September 1843 revolution, was the young King Otto forced to grant a constitution (Fig. 2.1).

The first constitution of the Kingdom of Greece was promulgated on 18 March 1844, turning the country into a constitutional monarchy. While parliamentary elections were first held in summer 1844, it took decades before concrete steps towards the full and effective introduction of a parliamentary system and the emergence of the prime minister as a key power holder were made. The 1862 expulsion of King Otto was followed by the arrival of King George I from the royal house of Glücksburg and the promulgation of a new constitution in 1864. This provided the framework for an incipient Westminster-style parliamentary system in the 1870s, under the leadership of Charilaos Trikoupis. The king became obliged to appoint as prime minister the leader of the party with the strongest parliamentary representation.[2] Greece was

Fig. 2.1 The 3 September 1843 Revolution-Colonel Dimitrios Kallergis demands a constitution from King Otto and Queen Amalia (Unknown artist, Museum of the City of Athens, Vouros-Eutaxias Foundation, Athens)

consolidating its position in the European state system as a British ally, and this facilitated the emergence of a British-style parliamentarism. Yet the political, social and diplomatic conditions of the late nineteenth century did not allow for quick steps, and the consolidation of Greek democracy would take longer than many would expect. Greece's painful economic default in 1893 and disastrous defeat against the Ottoman Empire in the 1897 war determined the political and diplomatic agenda of the country. Meanwhile, also due to the recurrent mobilizations, military influence upon politics increased, and coups became an increasingly common feature of Greek politics.[3] A perennial, internecine debate about the monarchical or republican character of the regime became intertwined with the recurring coups and was further punctuated by the country's participation in consecutive wars. War, coups and the conflict between monarchists and republicans left a heavy burden on Greek politics and society.

Yet a major constitutional overhaul had to wait until the aftermath of the 1909 Goudi military coup. The parliamentary elections

of 11 December (O.S. 28 November) 1910[4] and the meteoric rise of
Eleftherios Venizelos, a politician that came from the island of Crete to
promote a reformist agenda and eventually dominate Greek politics for
more than two decades,[5] facilitated the rise of a constitutional debate.
Contrary to the expectations of many of his supporters, Venizelos
rejected the calls for the introduction of republicanism, as he considered
the monarchy to be a crucial cementing factor in Greece. On the other
hand, the overhaul of the 1864 constitutional text was substantial: Fifty-
four articles were amended. While maintaining the monarchical character
of the regime, the 1911 Constitution put forward a series of reforms that
brought the Kingdom of Greece in line with the norm in most European
states of its era.

Nevertheless, the restoration of the political role of the king would
pave the ground for a series of political crises. The Balkan Wars (1912–
1913), the First World War (1914–1918), the Greek-Turkish War
(1919–1922), its subsequent population exchange and concomitant
political turmoil left a heavy imprint on Greek politics and formed the
background of a mounting conflict between the new King Constantine I
and Prime Minister Venizelos. Political polarization reached the level of a
constitutional crisis in 1915, when Constantine forced Venizelos into resignation twice in a year due to foreign policy disagreements, in particular
Greece's entry into the First World War on the side of the Entente. The
crisis peaked in August 1916 with the emergence of two governments,
one in Athens under the influence of the King and one in Thessaloniki
under the influence of Venizelos and the support of the Entente forces.
The Venizelos government managed to prevail with Entente support in
June 1917, after Greece had reached the verge of an outright civil war.

Constitutional debates often rotated around the question of monarchy vs. republicanism, due to the power struggle between King
Constantine I and Prime Minister Venizelos. A first of a series of referendums on the monarchical or republican character of the regime was held
in 1924 and was won by the republicans. The Second Hellenic Republic[6]
was promulgated with the 1925 Constitution. It lasted for 11 years
amidst recurring military coups, until a new referendum in 1935 restored
the monarchy and the 1864/1911 Constitution.[7] On 4 August 1936,
Ioannis Metaxas led yet another coup and suspended with the consent
of King George II several articles of the constitution. Metaxas' military
regime ruled over Greece until its occupation by German military forces
in April–May 1941. Greece's tripartite (German, Italian and Bulgarian)

occupation ended in October 1944, but this did not mean a return to constitutional normalcy. In the end of the Second World War, Greece emerged as a member of the Western democratic camp, but only after having suffered a catastrophic three-year civil war, which left its traces upon its political regime and social fabric.[8] The 1946–1949 civil war did not only result in immense human loss and economic destruction. No national reconciliation followed suit, and the Greek left faced persecution and discrimination. This reinforced divisions within the Greek society and provided crucial symbolic resources for the polarization of Greek politics for decades, obstructing the emergence of social consensus on critical political questions and fostering majoritarian views.[9]

Greece's membership of the Western alliance and the framing of the emerging Cold War as war between "freedom" and "tyranny" also meant that Greece's return to democracy in the aftermath of the Second World War was imperative. Nevertheless, the 1952 constitution reflected the illiberal reality of its times; it remained formally democratic; yet its provisions were undermined by a body of extraordinary legislation, the *"parasyntagma"* or "parallel constitution", a remnant of the Civil War era that crucially undermined the rule of law and democracy. While the constitution referred to the protection of individual rights and the democratic nature of the regime, in practice human rights were often compromised to the interest of "national security" or "state interest". Despite its NATO membership in 1953, Greek democracy remained procedural, while its civil society faced severe institutional limitations[10]: Persecution of leftist dissidents, deportations and imprisonments were common, while mistrust about the free and fair character of parliamentary elections was also widespread. The ban of KKE, Greece's Communist Party, and severe limitations to freedom of expression were coupled by the tutelary role played by the Palace in collaboration with the military and civil bureaucracy. Palace interventions led into political crises with Prime Minister Konstantinos Karamanlis in 1961 and Georgios Papandreou in 1965.[11] Political instability was used as a pretext for yet another military coup on 21 April 1967, which led to a seven-year junta regime. This coup was meant to have a deeper impact on Greek politics. In Latin American style, the colonels that led decided to rule over the country themselves, instead of ruling from behind by withdrawing from the political scene and installing entrusted politicians. During the seven years of the military regime, several attempts were made to introduce majoritarian elements with the aim to mitigate international criticism about the undemocratic nature of the regime. Populism was widely applied by the junta, as the regime claimed to represent the "true interests" of the Greek people against its "morally corrupt" elites, which were responsible for Greece's "plight". Constitutional politics was one of the instruments the military regime used. Following the abortive attempt of King Constantine II to overthrow the military regime in December 1967 and his subsequent exile, the colonels appointed a regent, and Colonel Georgios Papadopoulos became prime minister. Within a few months, they submitted a draft of a new constitution to referendum. In the new constitution of May 1968, the military was bestowed upon a tutelary role, while fundamental rights and freedoms were further curtailed. In July 1973, following a second abortive counter-coup, Papadopoulos decided to depose King Constantine II whom he considered the mastermind of both anti-junta plots and turn Greece into a presidential republic with himself as a strong head of state and the executive. The new constitution introduced key majoritarian elements such as the direct election of the president and was put into a new referendum in July 1973, as the junta hoped to gain popular legitimacy.[12]

Nevertheless, the November 1973 overthrow of Papadopoulos by a group of his colleagues under Brigadier General Dimitrios Ioannidis led to the suspension of constitutional plans and the military rule of the country until July 1974. A humiliating military defeat in Cyprus following an instigated coup against the Makarios government and the subsequent Turkish invasion of the island on 20 July 1974 brought an abrupt end to Greece's military regime. The new government under Prime Minister Konstantinos Karamanlis had to restore the foundations of the Greek democracy. Through a referendum on 8 December 1974, monarchy was abolished, and a new constitution was promulgated on 11 June 1975.

DEMOCRATIZATION REFORMS—THE ROLE OF THE CONSTITUTION

The advent of democracy in Southern Europe signalled a critical juncture in the democratization waves that swept through the European continent following the end of the Second World War. The trials of the military regime leaders pointed at the need to deliver justice while maintaining the rule of law[13] and aiming at breaking the vicious circle of polarization and retribution.

Since shedding the vestiges of authoritarianism was one of the primary aims of the new democratic regimes, majoritarianism became a key item of the political debate and coincided with the rise of populism. Since the restoration of "popular sovereignty" against "corrupt elites" was a key political demand, it was often conflated with the introduction of majoritarian elements into Greece's democratic regime. The Panhellenic Socialist Movement (*Panellinio Sosialistiko Kinima*-PASOK), a left-wing party founded by Andreas Papandreou on 3 September 1974, would fast rise into a dominant position in Greek politics, with a populist agenda featuring majoritarian elements.[14]

This debate featured highly in the parliamentary deliberations before the promulgation of the 1975 Constitution and peaked in 1985, when the PASOK government put forward a constitutional amendment aiming to trim the powers of the president in favour of these of the prime minister and promote a more majoritarian model of Greek democracy. The vision of achieving "pure and complete popular sovereignty" through the elimination of executive powers as well as the balancing role of the president against the prime minister was presented as an indispensable consequence of the completion of the democratic consolidation process.

The deliberation about the new constitution was a central one in the context of transition.[15] The attack against Greek democracy was attributed to the antidemocratic activities of the Palace and key elements of the bureaucracy. While the republican character of the Greek state was decided by referendum, the reestablishment of Greek democracy on firm grounds would be enacted through a new constitution. The elimination of the tutelary functions of the military and civil bureaucracy was one of the main aims of the constitutional drafters. On the other hand, this did not mean that populist majoritarianism was favoured by all political parties. The Karamanlis administration did not intend to destroy existing bureaucratic structures in the name of democratization[16] and aspired to build Greece's democratic regime on a delicate balance between the two heads of the executive, the prime minister and the president. While a parliamentary system was introduced, and the president was elected by qualified parliamentary majority, the president maintained considerable powers. Among the most significant powers, one could list the following:

a. dissolve the Parliament, if he considered that its composition was in apparent disharmony with popular feelings or could not secure government stability (Article 41§1);
b. dissolve the government when at his discretion there was no parliamentary majority (Article 38§2);
c. convene the council of ministers under extraordinary circumstances (Article 42);
d. ratify voted bills by the Parliament and refer back to the Parliament passed bills that he disagreed with (Article 42);
e. declare a referendum on critical political issues, regardless of the intentions of the government majority (Article 42).[17]

These provisions underlined that Prime Minister Karamanlis and his incumbent New Democracy (*Nea Dimokratia*-ND) party did not view Greece's transition to democracy as a complete victory of populism and an opportunity to turn Greek democracy towards majoritarianism. While the country's Westminster-type parliamentary tradition was preserved, the powers granted to the president aimed to recalibrate the balance between the executive, the legislative and the judiciary[18] and prevent the rise of an omnipotent prime minister who could accumulate executive and legislative powers without any restraint. A balance between the two heads of the executive, the president and the prime minister, was meant to deter power concentration in the hands of either.

Yet this choice of the Karamanlis administration met with the vocal opposition of the left-wing parties that formed the minority of the parliament and participated in the constitutional deliberations. The Panhellenic Socialist Movement (*Panellinio Sosialistiko Kinima*-PASOK) and the Communist Party of Greece (*Kommounistiko Komma Ellados*-KKE) argued that these provisions comprised a threat against the democratic nature of the regime and warned about the possibility of a top-level institutional crisis, if the views of the president and the prime minister differed on critical issues. Hence, they voiced their preference for a weaker, virtually ceremonial president and a stronger parliament and prime minister. As the leftist parties in the constitutional deliberations expressed their opposition to the balancing role of the president and advocated the full transfer of his powers to the parliament and the government, their argument was firmly based on a majoritarian view of politics. In their view, all powers should reside with the parliamentary majority and the government. They also aimed to limit the powers of state bureaucracy and advocated a more thorough purge of military regime sympathizers, in contrast to the rather moderate approach of the conservative government.[19] This appeared to pose a risk of conflict, which had cost Greece dearly in the past. Despite these views, the conservative Karamanlis government insisted on the promulgation of a constitution that aimed to establish a checks-and-balances system between the president and the prime minister. Despite the parliamentary nature of the Greek democracy, the president retained crucial powers, which could play a balancing role against the government and the prime minister.

When the new constitution came into force in 1975, there was slim chance to check whether the new constitution harboured the potential of a conflict between the two heads of the executive, the president and the prime minister. President Konstantinos Tsatsos was elected with the support of the incumbent New Democracy party, and hence the probability of him clashing with Prime Minister Konstantinos Karamanlis on key political issues was very low. Karamanlis himself was elected president in 1980 and would become the first president to test the functionality of the new constitution. In the parliamentary elections of 18 October 1981, the socialist PASOK, led by Andreas Papandreou, scored a historic victory collecting 48.1% of the vote and formed a single-party government.[20] The cohabitation of President Konstantinos Karamanlis and Prime Minister Andreas Papandreou was expected to produce recurrent, major political crises, given their deep ideological and political differences. Papandreou objected to Greece's membership of NATO and its recently accomplished accession to the European Economic Community (EEC). He suggested an alternative "third way" to achieve Greece's democratic and socialist transformation. In his rhetoric, no real democracy had been established in 1974, because the people were not truly empowered. The state elite which was responsible for the persecution of left-wing Greeks and contributed to the establishment and viability of the military regime was perceived to be the "enemy" still remaining in charge of the country. Only through the advent of PASOK to power would these elites lose their tutelary role, and true democracy be established. In that view, the bitter legacy of the military regime and the 1974 Cyprus crisis necessitated the dominant role of *volonté générale*, which was expressed by the incumbent party. In typical populist jargon, Papandreou argued that PASOK signed a "contract" with the "Greek people" thus claiming a unique and unprecedented affinity in Greek political history; PASOK was destined to fulfil the *volonté générale*, and this supreme and unfettered goal came to the point of intolerance to the voices of non-elected bodies, or to bodies governed through seniority and merit, as opposed through explicitly majoritarian outcomes.[21]

Yet, despite this background and contrary to what many had expected, no constitutional crisis was observed. Papandreou abandoned most of its radical electoral promises, such as Greece's withdrawal from the European Economic Community (EEC) and NATO, and maintained Greece's Western and European orientation.[22] On his part, President Karamanlis abstained from using his veto powers against a series of comprehensive legislative reforms introduced by PASOK, which realized some of its electoral promises, in the direction of empowering the people against business and state elites.[23] This even referred to the dilution of the power of state bureaucracy and the inclusion of party clients.[24] A *modus vivendi* was apparently achieved; checks and balances seemed to be working smoothly, and this rendered good services to Greek political stability.

NOTES

1. Arend Lijphart, *Patterns of Democracy: Government Forms and Performance in Thirty-Six Countries* (New Haven, CT: Yale University Press, 1999), p. 54.
2. John S. Koliopoulos and Thanos M. Veremis, *Modern Greece: A History since 1821* (Chichester: Wiley-Blackwell, 2010), pp. 44–46.
3. On the role of the military in Greek politics, see Thanos Veremis, *The Military in Greek Politics: From Independence to Democracy* (Montreal, New York & London: Blackrose Books, 1997).
4. Greece officially applied the Julian calendar in 1923, when 16 February moved to 1 March.
5. For more on the work and vision of Eleftherios Venizelos, see Paschalis M. Kitromilides, *Eleftherios Venizelos: The Trials of Statesmanship* (Edinburgh: Edinburgh University Press, 2008).
6. Revolutionary Greece was considered as the First Hellenic Republic, given the republican character of all three revolutionary constitutions.
7. Nicos C. Alivizatos, Το Σύνταγμα και οι Εχθροί του στη Νεοελληνική Ιστορία 1800–2010 [*The Constitution and its Enemies in Modern Greek History 1800–2010*] (Athens: Πόλις [Polis], 2011).
8. John S. Koliopoulos and Thanos Veremis, *Greece, the Modern Sequel: From 1821 to the Present* (London: Hurst & Co., 2002), pp. 68–98.

9. Richard Clogg, *A Concise History of Greece* (Cambridge: Cambridge University Press, 1992), pp. 145–150.

10. Nicos P. Mouzelis and George Pagoulatos, "Civil Society and Citizenship in Postwar Greece" in Faruk Birtek and Thalia Dragonas, eds., *Citizenship and the Nation State in Greece and Turkey* (London & New York: Routledge, 2005), pp. 88–92.

11. Nicos C. Alivizatos, *Οι Πολιτικοί Θεσμοί σε Κρίση 1922–1974: Όψεις της Ελληνικής Εμπειρίας [Political Institutions under Crisis: Aspects of the Greek Experience]* (Athens: Θεμέλιο [Themelio], 1995).

12. Alivizatos, *Το Σύνταγμα και οι Εχθροί του στη Νεοελληνική Ιστορία 1800–2010 [The Constitution and its Enemies in Modern Greek History 1800–2010]*, p. 665.

13. Nicos C. Alivizatos and P. Nikiforos Diamandouros, "Politics and the Judiciary in the Greek Transition to Democracy" in A. James McAdams, ed., *Transitional Justice and the Rule of Law in New Democracies* (Notre Dame and London: University of Notre Dame Press, 1997).

14. Both the choice of the word "movement" and not "party" and the foundation of the party on the anniversary of Greece's first constitutional revolution of 3 September 1843 were deliberate moves to strengthen PASOK's populist character.

15. On this, see P. Nikiforos Diamandouros, "Transition to, and Consolidation of, Democratic Politics in Greece, 1974–1983: A Tentative Assessment", *West European Politics*, Vol. 7, no. 2 (1984).

16. Dimitri A. Sotiropoulos, "Old Problems and New Challenges: The Enduring and Changing Functions of Southern European State Bureaucracies" in Richard Gunther, P. Nikiforos Diamandouros and Dimitri A. Sotiropoulos, eds., *Democracy and the State in the New Southern Europe* (Oxford: Oxford University Press, 2006), pp. 204–205.

17. Kostas Mavrias, "*Οι Αναθεωρήσεις του Συντάγματος του 1975* [The Amendments of the 1975 Constitution]" in Hellenic Parliament [Βουλή των Ελλήνων], ed., *30 Χρόνια από το Σύνταγμα του 1975: Τα Ελληνικά Συντάγματα από το Ρήγα Έως Σήμερα [30 Years from the 1975 Constitution: Greek Constitutions from Rigas until Today]* (Athens: Hellenic Parliament [Βουλή των Ελλήνων], 2005), pp. 233–239.

18. On the role of judiciary in Greek democratization process, see Alivizatos and Diamandouros, "Politics and the Judiciary in the Greek Transition to Democracy".

19. Dimitri A. Sotiropoulos, "The Authoritarian Past and Contemporary Greek Democracy", *South European Society and Politics*, Vol. 15, no. 3 (2010), pp. 457–458.

20. On the impact of PASOK on state–society relations in Greece, see Nikiforos P. Diamandouros, "Pasok and State-Society Relations in

Post-Authoritarian Greece, 1974–1988" in Speros Vryonis Jr., ed., *Greece on the Road to Democracy: From the Junta to Pasok* (New York: Aristide D. Caratzas, 1974).
21. For an excellent account of the transformation and the challenges that PASOK faced, see Yannis Voulgaris, *Η Ελλάδα της Μεταπολίτευσης 1974–1990 [Greece of the Transition 1974–1990]* (Athens: Θεμέλιο [Themelio], 2001).
22. On the transformation of early third-worldist PASOK to a less radical government party, see Michalis Spourdalakis and Chrisanthos Tassis, "Party Change in Greece and the Vanguard Role of Pasok", *South European Society and Politics*, Vol. 11, no. 3 (2006), pp. 497–501.
23. For example, legislation, which introduced the participation of labor unions in the management of "strategic" state-owned enterprises (SOEs), was justified on the grounds of serving "national interest and the social whole" and of enlisting SOEs in the struggle that PASOK had ostensibly launched against Greece's domestic political and economic elite and its Western patrons. In the field of higher education, PASOK aimed to turn faculty unions and the student movement from outsiders to key stakeholders in its aim to "socialize the state". Thus, majoritarian views spread within Greek higher education, inhibiting the administrative autonomy of universities, which came under the control of political parties, and harming academic pluralism and freedoms, as views opposing the dominant paradigm were barely tolerated. See, respectively, Demetrios B. Papoulias and Spyros Lioukas, "Participation in the Management of Public Enterprises: Experience from Greek Utilities", *Annals of Public and Cooperative Economics*, Vol. 66, no. 3 (1995) and Ioannis N. Grigoriadis and Antonis Kamaras, "Reform Paradoxes: Academic Freedom and Governance in Greek and Turkish Higher Education", *Southeast European and Black Sea Studies*, Vol. 12, no. 1 (2012), p. 140.
24. Sotiropoulos, "Old Problems and New Challenges: The Enduring and Changing Functions of Southern European State Bureaucracies".

REFERENCES

Nicos C. Alivizatos and P. Nikiforos Diamandouros, "Politics and the Judiciary in the Greek Transition to Democracy" in A. James McAdams, ed., *Transitional Justice and the Rule of Law in New Democracies* (Notre Dame and London: University of Notre Dame Press, 1997), pp. 27–60.
Nicos C. Alivizatos, *Οι Πολιτικοί Θεσμοί σε Κρίση 1922–1974: Όψεις της Ελληνικής Εμπειρίας [Political Institutions under Crisis: Aspects of the Greek Experience]* (Athens: Θεμέλιο [Themelio], 1995).

————, *Το Σύνταγμα και οι Εχθροί του στη Νεοελληνική Ιστορία 1800–2010* *[The Constitution and its Enemies in Modern Greek History 1800–2010]* (Athens: Πόλις [Polis], 2011).

Richard Clogg, *A Concise History of Greece* (Cambridge: Cambridge University Press, 1992).

Nikiforos P. Diamandouros, "Pasok and State-Society Relations in Post-Authoritarian Greece, 1974–1988" in Speros Vryonis Jr., ed., *Greece on the Road to Democracy: From the Junta to Pasok* (New York: Aristide D. Caratzas, 1974), pp. 15–35.

Nikiforos P. Diamandouros, "Transition to, and Consolidation of, Democratic Politics in Greece, 1974–1983: A Tentative Assessment", *West European Politics*, Vol. 7, no. 2 (1984), pp. 50–71.

Ioannis N. Grigoriadis and Antonis Kamaras, "Reform Paradoxes: Academic Freedom and Governance in Greek and Turkish Higher Education", *Southeast European and Black Sea Studies*, Vol. 12, no. 1 (2012), pp. 135–152.

Paschalis M. Kitromilides, *Eleftherios Venizelos: The Trials of Statesmanship* (Edinburgh: Edinburgh University Press, 2008).

John S. Koliopoulos and Thanos Veremis, *Greece, the Modern Sequel: From 1821 to the Present* (London: Hurst & Co., 2002).

John S. Koliopoulos and Thanos M. Veremis, *Modern Greece: A History since 1821* (Chichester: Wiley-Blackwell, 2010).

Arend Lijphart, *Patterns of Democracy: Government Forms and Performance in Thirty-Six Countries* (New Haven, CT: Yale University Press, 1999).

Kostas Mavrias, "Οι Αναθεωρήσεις του Συντάγματος του 1975 [The Amendments of the 1975 Constitution]" in Hellenic Parliament [Βουλή των Ελλήνων], ed., *30 Χρόνια από το Σύνταγμα του 1975: Τα Ελληνικά Συντάγματα από το Ρήγα Έως Σήμερα [30 Years from the 1975 Constitution: Greek Constitutions from Rigas until Today]* (Athens: Hellenic Parliament [Βουλή των Ελλήνων], 2005), pp. 233–266.

Nicos P. Mouzelis and George Pagoulatos, "Civil Society and Citizenship in Postwar Greece" in Faruk Birtek and Thalia Dragonas, eds., *Citizenship and the Nation State in Greece and Turkey* (London & New York: Routledge, 2005), pp. 87–103.

Demetrios B. Papoulias and Spyros Lioukas, "Participation in the Management of Public Enterprises: Experience from Greek Utilities", *Annals of Public and Cooperative Economics*, Vol. 66, no. 3 (1995), pp. 275–298.

Dimitri A. Sotiropoulos, "The Authoritarian Past and Contemporary Greek Democracy", *South European Society and Politics*, Vol. 15, no. 3 (2010), pp. 449–465.

————, "Old Problems and New Challenges: The Enduring and Changing Functions of Southern European State Bureaucracies" in Richard Gunther, P. Nikiforos Diamandouros and Dimitri A. Sotiropoulos, eds., *Democracy and the State in the New Southern Europe* (Oxford: Oxford University Press, 2006), pp. 197–234.

Michalis Spourdalakis and Chrisanthos Tassis, "Party Change in Greece and the Vanguard Role of Pasok", *South European Society and Politics*, Vol. 11, no. 3 (2006), pp. 497–512.

Thanos Veremis, *The Military in Greek Politics: From Independence to Democracy* (Montreal, New York & London: Blackrose Books, 1997).

Yannis Voulgaris, *Η Ελλάδα της Μεταπολίτευσης 1974–1990 [Greece of the Transition 1974–1990]* (Athens: Θεμέλιο [Themelio], 2001).

CHAPTER 3

Democratic Transition in Turkey

Abstract The roots of Turkey's constitutional history are found in the late years of the Ottoman Empire and the 1876 Ottoman Constitution. The first republican constitution in 1924 set a preference for a parliamentary system, however majoritarian pressures have existed since the advent of multi-party politics. The 1982 Constitution prioritized state interests over human rights and came under heavy pressure during the 1999–2005 democratization process. While the AKP first spearheaded the introduction of a liberal democratic constitution, it later shifted its interest in promoting a majoritarian shift reinforcing the powers of the president.

Keywords AKP · Atatürk · Erdoğan · Democratization · Military coup

INTRODUCTION

Like many aspects of Turkish politics, constitution-making in the late Ottoman Empire and republican Turkey has been a top-down process. Constitutions have most commonly emerged as a result of revolutions and military coups and have not relied upon societal and political deliberation and participatory institutions. The absence of a deliberative legacy helps explain why a majoritarian understanding of democracy has become a dominant feature of republican constitutions.[1]

© The Author(s) 2018   27
I.N. Grigoriadis, *Democratic Transition and the Rise of Populist Majoritarianism*, Reform and Transition in the Mediterranean,
DOI 10.1007/978-3-319-57556-8_3

Turkey has followed a longer and more arduous path towards democratic consolidation than Greece. The coup of 12 September 1980 reversed any prior democratization steps and singled Turkey out from other Southern European states that were experiencing a transition to democracy in the 1970s. The establishment of a military regime from 1980 to 1983 and the tutelary role of the military guaranteed by the 1982 Constitution meant that Turkey's drive towards democratization was irrevocably decoupled from that of other southern European states. Major steps toward democratic consolidation were realized almost twenty years later, when Turkey's candidacy for membership of the European Union triggered a virtuous circle of political reform that lasted from 1999 to 2005. While democratization reform started losing impetus in 2005, a showdown between the government and the military in 2007 and the judiciary in 2008 resulted in the complete civilianization of Turkish politics and the virtual elimination of the tutelary role which military and civilian bureaucracy had enjoyed for decades. Following a series of judicial investigations, scores of army officers—including generals— were detained, facing charges of conspiracy against the government and coup plotting. The democratically elected, populist conservative government of the Justice and Development Party (*Adalet ve Kalkınma Partisi- AKP*) appeared to be in full charge. On the other hand, rising concerns about the authoritarian tendencies of the government were coupled with the publication of constitutional amendment plans that would sharply reinforce the majoritarian elements in Turkey's democratic regime. The abortive coup of 15 July 2016 and its aftermath highlighted the threats Turkish democracy was still facing. It also pointed at the dire need to steer constitutional reform towards building strong democratic institutions able to unite divergent segments of Turkish society through consensus building. With a time lag of 30 years from Greece, majoritarianism acquired a key position in the agenda of Turkish politics.

CONSTITUTIONAL HISTORY

If we seek the roots of Turkish constitutionalism in the late Ottoman Empire, the 1808 Deed of Alliance (*Sened-i İttifak*), The 1839 Imperial Rescript of the Rose Garden (*Hatt-i Şerif-i Gülhane*) and the 1856 Reform Imperial Rescript (*Islahat Hatt-ı Hümayun or Fermanı*) were the first steps towards the establishment of an Ottoman constitutional order. All three documents included provisions that would normally be

Fig. 3.1 The Ottoman Parliament (Meclis-i Mebusan) reconvenes following the 1908 Young Turk Revolution and the Restoration of the Constitution

found in a constitutional text. Nevertheless, in all three documents there were no real limitations to the power of the Sultan: The implementation of declarations about the protection of subject rights, just and fair administration remained at his discretion. The Ottoman Empire would acquire its first fully fledged constitution in 1876, following the deposition of Sultan Abdülaziz and the rise to power of Sultan Murat V. The 1876 constitution authors hoped that the introduction of an Ottoman constitution and the protection of fundamental rights would deter the centrifugal forces in the Ottoman Empire; they did not go, however, as far as to introduce a constitutional monarchy. The Sultan remained sovereign, yet a bicameral assembly was for the first time introduced. While the Senate members were to be appointed for life by the Sultan, the members of the Chamber of Deputies (*Meclis-i Mebusan*) were to be indirectly elected by property-owning Ottoman subjects[2] (Fig. 3.1).

Nevertheless, even these hesitant steps for the establishment of a constitutional order were not destined to last for long. Sultan Murat V was considered mentally unfit, and his successor Sultan Abdülhamid II took the opportunity of the 1877–1878 Russian–Ottoman war to suspend the constitution and purge reformist bureaucrats. Abdülhamid II's auto-cratic rule lasted for more than 30 years. On 24 July 1908, Ottoman military units stationed in the Balkans revolted demanding a restoration of the 1876 Constitution, and the Sultan had to accept their demand. The Young Turk Revolution was bestowed with many hopes, as con-stitutionalism was perceived by many as the last chance for the survival of the Ottoman Empire as an intact political unit. Despite initial opti-mism and the amendments of the 1876 constitution towards stronger protection of human rights and introduction of a parliamentary system, the restoration of the constitution proved short-lived. While the new constitutional regime survived an abortive counterrevolution in April 1909, it came under increasing pressure due to unfavourable for the Ottoman Empire political developments. In the end, the Balkan Wars provided a pretext for the discontinuation of the constitu-tional order, as yet another "state of emergency" was declared. The 23 January 1913 military coup took place between the First and the Second Balkan War, which led to the rise of the triumvirate of Enver, Talat and Cemal Paşa and the suspension of the constitution. The Triumvirate led the Ottoman Empire to the fateful decision to enter the First World War on the side of the Central Empires. Following the Moudros Armistice of 30 October 1918, the Ottoman Empire capitulated, and Istanbul was occupied by Entente forces. While the Ottoman government came under the control of the allies, Turkish nationalist opposition led by Mustafa Kemal moved to Ankara, established a new parliament there on 24 April 1920 and vowed to repel invading forces. This led to the emergence of two competing authorities in the remaining Ottoman territories. Slowly gaining international legitimacy, the Ankara government introduced a wartime constitution or "Law of Fundamental *Organization*" (*Teşkilât-ı Esasiye Kanunu*) on 20 January 1921. This was a rather laconic text: It avoided addressing the position of the Sultan who remained in occu-pied Istanbul and aimed to respond to the basic needs of an incipient state in a military emergency. Yet the 1921 Constitution did proclaim in its twenty-one articles the principle of national sovereignty and vested legislative and executive powers to the Assembly. It represented a typi-cal example of the assembly government model, where the ministers depended on the confidence of the assembly, while the government had no power to dissolve the assembly.[3]

The Sultan remained the head of the state, as Mustafa Kemal avoided addressing the divisive issue of republicanism under the sensitive war conditions. The victorious for the Ankara government end of the war in August–September 1922, the abolition of the sultanate on 1 November 1922 and the departure of the last Sultan Mehmet VI Vahdettin from Istanbul to exile, the signature of the Treaty of Lausanne on 24 July 1923, the declaration of the Republic on 29 October 1923 and the abolition of the caliphate on 3 March 1924 drew the framework for the new Turkish constitution.

Mustafa Kemal was the president of the young Republic, the leader of the Republican People's Party (*Cumhuriyet Halk Partisi*-CHP) and already the towering figure of Turkish politics. Most of the conservative politicians that objected to his rule and were influential between 1919 and 1923 had eclipsed. Yet his dominance had not yet reached the levels it would after 1925, when Turkey was effectively transformed into a single-party system. The new constitution did not eliminate the powers of the legislative in favour of the executive and the president. It did feature, however, a populist majoritarian understanding of democracy, where the legislature represents the *volonté générale* of the sovereign nation and limited protection for human rights and freedoms. As no room was harboured for dissenting views and minorities, the 1924 Constitution did not prove a major obstacle to the authoritarian transformation of the Turkish Republic. After 1925, Mustafa Kemal was able to consolidate his power grip and silence all opposition, be it ethnic, religious or ideological. The president de facto exercised all the powers of the assembly and became the undisputed head of the executive and the authentic interpreter of the *volonté générale*. This eventually allowed him to launch his radical political reform aiming to raise Turkey to the standards of "contemporary civilization (*muasır medeniyet*)".[4]

A preference for a parliamentary system was one of the key features of republican Turkish constitutions. Ever since the first constitution of republican Turkey was promulgated in 1924, the legislative has acquired a key position in power sharing. Yet majoritarianism has been a feature whose weight has vacillated depending on the socio-political circumstances. In the first republican constitution of 1924, majoritarianism featured strongly.[5] The legislative was keen on not empowering the executive or the judiciary with powers that would balance its own. The proposal to give the president the power to dissolve the parliament was rejected. Nevertheless, as Turkey entered a single-party era soon thereafter, these distinctions bore little importance. The advent of multiparty politics of 1946 and the rise of the Democrat Party (*Demokrat*

Parti-DP) in 1950 led to a political environment, which strained the relations between the government and the bureaucracy. The intention of the Adnan Menderes administration to consolidate the majoritarian character of the republic, eliminate existing checks and balances and persecute dissent was one of the contributing factors to the military coup of 27 May 1960. Former oppressors suddenly became oppressed and former oppressed oppressors in a pattern that would be repeated in the coming decades.

The coup of 27 May 1960 put a violent end to the DP era and set out a new constitutional debate under the strict control of the military. Mitigating the majoritarian elements of the 1924 Constitution that allowed the DP government to gather excessive power through its control of the parliament and establishing a tutelary role for the Turkish military were two of the main objectives of the 1961 Constitution. The military introduced a constitution that espoused "attenuated parliamentarism" (*parlementarisme attenué*).[6] This was designed to preclude the possibility that a populist government might attempt to consolidate its unchecked rule by introducing a new constitution. The 1961 Constitution aimed to establish a system of checks and balances[7] which would obstruct the rise of a "tyranny of the majority", or else a "reserved democracy".[8] This included measures that promoted democratic institutions, as well as the guardian role of the bureaucratic elite. While the reinforcement of the judiciary through the introduction of a Constitutional Court as well as the principle of judicial review could be seen as an example of the first, the establishment of a National Security Council (*Milli Güvenlik Kurulu*-MGK) under the control of the military and with extensive executive powers in widely defined security issues clearly pointed at a tutelary role of bureaucratic institutions.[9] The guardian role of bureaucratic elite was meant to deter the relapse of majoritarian politics, which were named as the reason for the military involvement into politics. Hence, majoritarianism suffered a significant retreat, but so were the prospects for democratic consolidation. The country was ruled by a series of coalition governments, while its presidents were elected by the parliament and not by the people. As the liberal aspects of the 1961 Constitution contributed to a higher degree of polarization, the rise of a vibrant and at times violent political debate in Turkey gave the pretext for a second military coup on 12 March 1971. This culminated in constitutional reforms aiming to curb personal freedoms and reinforce the tutelary role of the civil and military bureaucracy. As this intervention failed to channel Turkish political developments and prevent the rise of Kurdish nationalism and a widening left–right political divide, a third military coup was organized on 12 September 1980. The 1980–1983 military regime attempted a deeper and more lasting transformation of Turkish politics and society through the introduction of a new illiberal constitution. The 1982 constitution and the return to civilian politics provided the ground for the gradual proliferation of populism and majoritarianism,[10] by idealizing the state, the people and giving excess powers to the head of the executive at the absence of any checks-and-balances mechanisms.

DEMOCRATIZATION REFORMS-THE ROLE OF THE CONSTITUTION

It is hard to overstate the significance of the 12 September 1980 coup for the course of constitutional politics and democratization in Turkey. Turkey was dissociated from the democratization wave that swept through Greece, Spain and Portugal in the 1970s, which was further reinforced and consolidated by their membership of the European Economic Community (EEC). The 1980–1983 Evren military regime dealt a heavy blow against human rights and democratic institutions, and reinforced majoritarian features. Most importantly, it made sure that its priorities would be raised into constitutional guidelines, before the return to civilian politics. In view of the above, when democratization reform gained political traction, it was inevitable that constitutional amendments would become a focal point. Improving EU–Turkey relations played a crucial role in a rising debate, which dominated Turkish politics between 1999 and 2005. Improving the quality of democratic institutions, protecting human rights and ending the tutelary role of the military and the civilian bureaucracy were issues that eventually were entangled with the debate on the majoritarian features of Turkish democracy.

The 1982 Constitution proved to be the most lasting legacy of the 1980–1983 military regime. It became a major obstacle to Turkey's path towards democratic consolidation and set an illiberal and state-centred backdrop against which all constitutional amendment efforts have been measured. In Özbudun's view, the 1982 Constitution reflected the "authoritarian, tutelary and statist mentality of its military founders and their deep distrust of civilian politics".[11] The existence of numerous and general constitutional limitations to fundamental rights and liberties was a manifestation of the statist mentality of the author of the constitutional text and a serious challenge to the effective protection of freedoms as important as these of expression, religion and association. The absence of full and effective protection of human rights was not the only issue. The balance between the president, the parliament, the government, the judiciary and other unelected bodies, which was protected by the 1961 Constitution, was disturbed in favour of the establishment of a tutelary regime, which included the president among its key instruments.[12] While all Turkish constitutions have recognized the parliament as the leading power holder in the Turkish political system, in practice its power has shifted to the executive, in particular the prime minister, and the judiciary, more specifically the Constitutional Court. In the view of Özbudun, the 1982 Constitution heralded a gradual transition from a purely parliamentary to an increasingly presidential model. Key powers were awarded to unelected bodies, such as the National Security Council (*Milli Güvenlik Kurulu*-MGK), while the power balance tilted from civilian bureaucratic towards military institutions. The president was also awarded additional powers with the aim to deter a relapse to the political confrontations that became the pretext for the 1980 military coup. This meant that the political system developed a *sui generis* nature, between parliamentarianism and presidentialism.[13] The military also secured exit guarantees, so its privileges would not be questioned following its withdrawal from active government.

Moreover, the 1982 Constitution focused on the reinforcement of the tutelary role of the judiciary. While the judiciary is normally the weakest of the three powers, it accumulated disproportionate powers in the context of the 1982 Constitution, with the aim to protect the tutelary functions and the institutional autonomy of the military and civil bureaucracy. The "activist role" of the judiciary became one of the most controversial features of Turkish politics, in particular with reference to the Constitutional Court. As Turkey's democratic consolidation process allowed for the rise to power of parties that originated from political Islam or were linked with the Kurdish nationalist movement, the Constitutional Court undertook the role of the guardian of the founding norms of the 1982 Constitution by evaluating the loyalty of such parties to the constitutional principles. Özbudun suggested that Hirschl's theory of "hegemonic preservation" may help clarify the attitude of the

Constitutional Court: political elites that were once dominant and now threatened by majoritarian politics might resort to judicial review of constitutionality as a means to prevent a state takeover.[14] This "judicial activism" was so pronounced, which led some to describe it as "juristocracy". One should not omit mentioning the centralized and non-transparent structure of the administration and the institutional autonomy which the military, the judiciary and segments of the civil bureaucracy have enjoyed, as a result of the exit guarantees that the 1980–1983 military regime had secured.

The unconditional prioritization of state stability and the clear mistrust that the constitution manifested against civil society, democratic politics and institutions led to mounting criticisms following the restoration of civilian politics.[15] Seventeen constitutional amendments from 1987 onwards aimed at the gradual reinforcement of human rights and the weakening of the tutelary character of the regime.[16] This mission gained traction after 1999, when Turkey became a candidate state for membership of the European Union. Turkey strived to fulfil the Copenhagen Criteria for EU membership through reform packages aiming to undermine the tutelary and antidemocratic character of the 1982 Constitution and contribute to the consolidation of Turkish democracy.[17]

On the other hand, the first signs for the rise of majoritarianism became evident. Moving away from the parliamentary towards a more majoritarian model emerged as one of the key items in the agenda of several governments. Unlike in Greece, the focal point of the battle about majoritarianism was not the reinforcement of the position of the Prime Minister. The president was the figure of the executive who was to benefit from the new balance in the separation of powers. Turgut Özal, Turkey's charismatic prime minister and president, advocated in the early 1990s a shift of the regime towards a semi-presidential system. Like Adnan Menderes in the 1950s, Turgut Özal found the existing system too limiting to his ambitions and argued for the dilution of checks and balances against the executive and the introduction of more elements of presidentialism in Turkey.[18]

While his plans failed to come to fruition, not least because he passed away unexpectedly, the question of strengthening the executive as an instrument of promoting political stability remained intact.[19] The issue would emerge again on occasions of constitutional reform debate.[20] His successor Süleyman Demirel also made occasional statements on the reinforcement of presidential powers.[21]

Awarding Turkey a candidate status for EU membership in December 1999 proved a catalyst for a series of democratization reforms that would shape the early 2000s. Both the DSP–ANAP–MHP coalition government under Bülent Ecevit and the AKP governments under Abdullah Gül and Recep Tayyip Erdoğan put forward ambitious reform programmes aiming to achieve the country convergence with the Copenhagen Criteria. This also involved far-reaching constitutional reform. Improving the quality of democratic institutions, protecting human rights, ending the tutelary role of the military and the civilian bureaucracy led to significant steps in the direction of democratic consolidation.[22] While improving the quality of democratic institutions also entailed the development of more effective checks-and-balances mechanisms, there was no direct discussion on the majoritarian features of Turkish democracy. In other words, the parliamentary system was considered to be providing a reasonable balance between the majoritarian and consensus elements of the Turkish democracy. This was clear in all constitutional debates, including those that led to the preparation in 2007 of a new draft constitution by an experts committee led by the professor of constitutional law Ergun Özbudun.

Only after the triumphant electoral victory of the AKP in June 2007 and the constitutional referendum of 2010 did the introduction of a presidential system become an integral element of Turkey's constitutional reform debates. Originating from Turkish political Islam, the AKP reinforced populist elements in its political agenda, presenting itself as the true representative of popular interests against state elites. This fitted well with a growing emphasis on majoritarianism. Eventually, the AKP interest shifted from the introduction of a new constitution which would meet the expectations of a consolidated liberal democracy to the introduction of a presidential system which would reinforce the majoritarian elements of Turkish democracy. This debate rose to the single most important item in the country's political agenda, as it was fixed to the personal ambitions of Recep Tayyip Erdoğan, the leading figure of Turkish politics at the outset of the new century. Meanwhile, the reform process was stalled, and Turkey was embroiled in consecutive domestic and international crises.[23]

The failure of the Kurdish peace process, the June 2013 Gezi demonstrations, the rising confrontation and eventual all-out war between the

AKP government and its former ally, the Gülen movement, the domestic effect of collapse of the regional order in the Middle East following the 2011 Arab uprisings, in particular in Syria, all contributed to the derailment of the democratic consolidation process. The direct election of Recep Tayyip Erdoğan to the presidency in August 2014 underscored his dominant role in Turkish politics[24] and accelerated the majoritarian shift of Turkish politics, as he intended to concentrate the executive power to the office of the president, even before a constitutional reform was held. Turkey started resembling again the model of "delegative" or "plebiscitarian democracy" that O'Donnell had developed for Latin America.[25] It ceased to be the role model for political and economic reform in the Mediterranean and the Middle East, and pluralist gains seemed to recede in favour of a religious conservative narrative of Turkish history and view of Turkish society.[26] Populism and majoritarian views dominated the government discourse, and constitutional reform was now framed in terms of introducing a strong presidential system. Nevertheless, especially in the aftermath of the abortive coup of 15 July 2016 and the declaration of a state of emergency, the debate moved beyond the realm of majoritarianism. Under these circumstances, scholars started interpreting developments as Turkey's drifting towards a competitive authoritarian system.[27]

NOTES

1. The 1961 constitution is an exception confirming the rule and is due to the political circumstances after the 27 May 1960 coup. See Ergun Özbudun, *The Constitutional System of Turkey: 1876 to the Present* (New York and London: Palgrave Macmillan, 2011), pp. 9–14.
2. Ibid., pp. 1–5.
3. Ibid., pp. 5–6.
4. Ibid., p. 8.
5. Ergun Özbudun and Ömer Faruk Gençkaya, *Democratization and the Politics of Constitution-Making in Turkey* (Budapest and New York: Central European University Press, 2009), pp. 12–13.
6. On this, see Levent Gönenç, "Presidential Elements in Government: Turkey", *European Constitutional Law Review*, Vol. 4, no. 3 (2008).
7. Aydın Yalçın, "Turkey: Emerging Democracy", *Foreign Affairs*, Vol. 45, no. 4 (1967), pp. 710–711.
8. Mustafa Erdoğan, *Türkiye'de Anayasalar ve Siyaset* (Ankara: Liberte, 2011), pp. 111–120.

9. On the role of tutelary institutions, see Ceren Lord, "The Persistence of Turkey's Majoritarian System of Government", *Government and Opposition*, Vol. 47, no. 2 (2012), pp. 253–254.

10. On the Turkish version of majoritarianism, see Paul Kubicek, "Majoritarian Democracy in Turkey" in Cengiz Erisen and Paul Kubicek, eds., *Democratic Consolidation in Turkey: Micro and Macro Challenges* (Oxford and New York: Routledge, 2016).

11. Özbudun, *The Constitutional System of Turkey: 1876 to the Present*, p. 37.

12. Erdoğan, *Türkiye'de Anayasalar ve Siyaset*, pp. 149–155.

13. Ergun Özbudun, "The Status of the President of the Republic under the Constitution of 1982: Presidentialism or Parliamentarism?" in Metin Heper and Ahmet Evin, eds., *State, Democracy and the Military: Turkey in the 1980s* (Berlin & New York: Walter de Gruyter, 1988), pp. 37–40.

14. Özbudun, *The Constitutional System of Turkey: 1876 to the Present*, pp. 122–124.

15. İlkay Sunar, *State, Society and Democracy in Turkey* (Istanbul: Bahçeşehir University Press, 2004), p. 109.

16. Ergun Özbudun, "Turkey's Search for a New Constitution", *Insight Turkey*, Vol. 14, no. 1 (2012), p. 43.

17. For more on this, see Ergun Özbudun, "Democratization Reforms in Turkey, 1993–2004", *Turkish Studies*, Vol. 8, no. 2 (2007).

18. Metin Heper and Menderes Çınar, "Parliamentary Government with a Strong President: The Post-1989 Turkish Experience", *Political Science Quarterly*, Vol. 111, no. 3 (1996), pp. 493–497.

19. See, for example, K. Haluk Yavuz, *Türkiye'de Siyasal Sistem Arayışı ve Yürütmenin Güçlendirilmesi* (Ankara: Seçkin, 2000).

20. Meltem Caniklioğlu, "Türkiye'nin Sistem Sorunu Mu Var?", *Kamu Hukuku Arşivi*, Vol. 2, no. 3 (1999), pp. 184–186.

21. On the debate of that era, see Betil Emrah Oder, "Türkiye'de Başkanlık ve Yarı Başkanlık Rejimi Tartışmaları: 1991–2005 Yılları Arasında Basına Yansıyan Öneri ve Tepkilerden Kesitler" in Teoman Ergül, ed., *Başkanlık Sistemi* (Ankara: Türkiye Barolar Birliği, 2005).

22. On Turkey's EU reform process, see Ioannis N. Grigoriadis, *Trials of Europeanization : Turkish Political Culture and the European Union*, 1st ed. (New York: Palgrave Macmillan, 2009), pp. 31–40 and Ioannis N. Grigoriadis, "Turkey's Accession to the European Union: Debating the Most Difficult Enlargement Ever", *SAIS Review of International Affairs*, Vol. 26, no. 1 (2006), pp. 149–153.

23. Ilter Turan, *Turkey's Difficult Journey to Democracy: Two Steps Forward, One Step Back* (Oxford: Oxford University Press, 2015), pp. 206–232.

24. Ergun Özbudun, "The 2014 Presidential Elections in Turkey: A Post-Election Analysis" in Senem Aydın-Düzgit, Daniela Huber, Meltem

Müftüler-Baç, E. Fuat Keyman, et al., eds., *Global Turkey in Europe III: Democracy, Trade, and the Kurdish Question in Turkey-EU Relations* (Rome: IAI and Edizioni Nuova Cultura, 2015), pp. 99–103.

25. Ergun Özbudun, "AKP at the Crossroads: Erdoğan's Majoritarian Drift", *South European Society and Politics*, Vol. 19, no. 2 (2014), pp. 162–163.

26. Onur Bakiner, "Is Turkey Coming to Terms with its Past? Politics of Memory and Majoritarian Conservatism", *Nationalities Papers*, Vol. 41, no. 5 (2013), pp. 700–702.

27. Berk Esen and Sebnem Gumuscu, "Rising Competitive Authoritarianism in Turkey", *Third World Quarterly*, Vol. 37, no. 9 (2016), pp. 1582–1584. On the concept of competitive authoritarianism, see Lucan A. Way and Steven Levitsky, "The Rise of Competitive Authoritarianism", *Journal of Democracy*, Vol. 13, no. 2 (2002).

References

Onur Bakiner, "Is Turkey Coming to Terms with its Past? Politics of Memory and Majoritarian Conservatism", Nationalities Papers, Vol. 41, no. 5 (2013), pp. 691–708.

Meltem Caniklioğlu, "Türkiye'nin Sistem Sorunu Mu Var?", *Kamu Hukuku Arşivi*, Vol. 2, no. 3 (1999), pp. 184–186.

Mustafa Erdoğan, *Türkiye'de Anayasalar ve Siyaset* (Ankara: Liberte, 2011).

Berk Esen and Sebnem Gumuscu, "Rising Competitive Authoritarianism in Turkey", *Third World Quarterly*, Vol. 37, no. 9 (2016), pp. 1581–1606.

Levent Gönenç, "Presidential Elements in Government: Turkey", *European Constitutional Law Review*, Vol. 4, no. 3 (2008), pp. 488–523.

Ioannis N. Grigoriadis, "Turkey's Accession to the European Union: Debating the Most Difficult Enlargement Ever", *SAIS Review of International Affairs*, Vol. 26, no. 1 (2006), pp. 147–160.

Ioannis N. Grigoriadis, *Trials of Europeanization : Turkish Political Culture and the European Union*, 1st ed. (New York: Palgrave Macmillan, 2009).

Metin Heper and Menderes Çınar, "Parliamentary Government with a Strong President: The Post-1989 Turkish Experience", *Political Science Quarterly*, Vol. 111, no. 3 (1996), pp. 483–503.

Paul Kubicek, "Majoritarian Democracy in Turkey" in Cengiz Erisen and Paul Kubicek, eds., *Democratic Consolidation in Turkey: Micro and Macro Challenges* (Oxford & New York: Routledge, 2016), pp. 123–143.

Ceren Lord, "The Persistence of Turkey's Majoritarian System of Government", *Government and Opposition*, Vol. 47, no. 2 (2012), pp. 228–255.

Betil Emrah Oder, "Türkiye'de Başkanlık ve Yarı Başkanlık Rejimi Tartışmaları: 1991–2005 Yılları Arasında Basına Yansıyan Öneri ve Tepkilerden Kesitler" in

Teoman Ergül, ed., *Başkanlık Sistemi* (Ankara: Türkiye Barolar Birliği, 2005), pp. 31–69.

Ergun Özbudun, "The Status of the President of the Republic under the Constitution of 1982: Presidentialism or Parliamentarism?" in Metin Heper and Ahmet Evin, eds., *State, Democracy and the Military: Turkey in the 1980s* (Berlin & New York: Walter de Gruyter, 1988), pp. 37–45.

Ergun Özbudun, "Democratization Reforms in Turkey, 1993–2004", *Turkish Studies*, Vol. 8, no. 2 (2007), pp. 179–196.

Ergun Özbudun and Ömer Faruk Gençkaya, *Democratization and the Politics of Constitution-Making in Turkey* (Budapest & New York: Central European University Press, 2009).

Ergun Özbudun, *The Constitutional System of Turkey: 1876 to the Present* (New York & London: Palgrave Macmillan, 2011).

Ergun Özbudun "Turkey's Search for a New Constitution", *Insight Turkey,* Vol. 14, no. 1 (2012), pp. 39–50.

Ergun Özbudun, "AKP at the Crossroads: Erdoğan's Majoritarian Drift", *South European Society and Politics,* Vol. 19, no. 2 (2014), pp. 155–167.

Ergun Özbudun, "The 2014 Presidential Elections in Turkey: A Post-Election Analysis" in Senem Aydın-Düzgit, Daniela Huber, Meltem Müftüler-Baç, E. Fuat Keyman, Michael Schwarz and Nathalie Tocci, eds., *Global Turkey in Europe III: Democracy, Trade, and the Kurdish Question in Turkey-EU Relations* (Rome: IAI & Edizioni Nuova Cultura, 2015), pp. 99–106.

İlkay Sunar, *State, Society and Democracy in Turkey* (Istanbul: Bahçeşehir University Press, 2004).

Ilter Turan, *Turkey's Difficult Journey to Democracy: Two Steps Forward, One Step Back* (Oxford: Oxford University Press, 2015).

Lucan A. Way and Steven Levitsky, "The Rise of Competitive Authoritarianism", *Journal of Democracy,* Vol. 13, no. 2 (2002), pp. 51–65.

Aydın Yalçın, "Turkey: Emerging Democracy", *Foreign Affairs,* Vol. 45, no. 4 (1967), pp. 706–714.

K. Haluk Yavuz, *Türkiye'de Siyasal Sistem Arayışı ve Yürütmenin Güçlendirilmesi* (Ankara: Seçkin, 2000).

CHAPTER 4

The Rising Tide of Populist Majoritarianism in Greece

Abstract The rising tide of populist majoritarianism in Greece can be reflected through the amendments of the 1975 constitution. The 1986 constitutional amendment allowed for an open discussion of the merits and weaknesses of reinforcing the majoritarian elements of Greek democracy. Similar discussions could be traced in the constitutional amendments of 2001 and 2008. The 2016 initiative of the SYRIZA–ANEL coalition government to launch a constitutional amendment process has brought once again majoritarianism to the forefront.

Keywords Majoritarianism · PASOK · Amendment SYRIZA · Papandreou · Tsipras · Greece

THE RISE OF PASOK

Post-1974 Greek politics have been characterized by populism and polarization—driven majoritarianism. The advent of majoritarianism in Greece has coincided with the political dominance of the Panhellenic Socialist Movement (PASOK), a party that emerged from the left of the Greek political spectrum and succeeded—largely thanks to the charismatic leadership of Andreas Papandreou in the 1980s first, and then thanks to the skilful management of Kostas Simitis in the late 1990s—to shape Greece's political and constitutional agenda. To meet its ends, PASOK extensively engaged in populist rhetoric by capitalizing on the symbolic

I.N. Grigoriadis, *Democratic Transition and the Rise of Populist Majoritarianism*, Reform and Transition in the Mediterranean, DOI 10.1007/978-3-319-57556-8_4 resources of the Second World War and Greece's 1941–1944 occupation, the 1946–1949 civil war, the post-Second World War oppression of the left, the 1967–1974 junta and the 1974 defeat in Cyprus. PASOK claimed to be the first party bringing "true democracy" to Greece by representing not the "state elite" interests as the right-wing parties were supposedly doing, but those of the Greek people, in particular its "non-privileged" middle and lower middle class. As following consecutive electoral successes PASOK was establishing its own clientelistic structures in the state bureaucracy, it continued the use of symbolic resources from the pool of pre-1981 Greek history with the aim to maintain its populist credentials against New Democracy intact.

When PASOK came to power following a resounding electoral victory in October 1981, many wondered whether it would keep its promises of withdrawing Greece from the European Economic Community (EEC), NATO and expelling US military bases from Greek territory. The presence of Konstantinos Karamanlis at the office of the president was seen as a crucial check and balance against such steps. While PASOK eventually backed off in almost all important promises made on its path to power, Papandreou decided to skilfully use the constitution in order to launch a symbolic confrontation with his political arch rival, President Karamanlis. Karamanlis used to be prime minister between 1974 and 1980, the historic leader of the Greek centre-right and the politician who successfully managed Greece's transition to democracy in summer 1974 despite Greece's military defeat in Cyprus. Through a majoritarian-leaning constitutional amendment proposal, Papandreou would revert to his populist toolkit in his aim to appease popular disillusionment about the first term of PASOK administration and win the popular vote in the upcoming parliamentary elections.

THE CONSTITUTIONAL AMENDMENT OF 1986

Konstantinos Karamanlis had moved from the office of the prime minister to that of the president in May 1980, a year and a half before the October 1981 elections that brought PASOK to power and Andreas Papandreou to the office of the prime minister. Despite initial concerns and PASOK's polarizing rhetoric, both Karamanlis and Papandreou cooperated without any major confrontation almost throughout their cohabitation. Yet this successful model of consensus would reach its end in 1985. Contrary to public expectations, Papandreou decided not to support the extension of Karamanlis' presidential tenure. He opted to support the candidacy of Christos Sartzetakis, a judge who had acquired fame in the 1960s due to his honest investigation of the 1963 assassination of Grigorios Lamprakis, a left-wing deputy against pressure from the security services. At the same time, Papandreou stated that he would put forward a constitutional amendment process with the aim to curb the "excessive" powers of the president.[1] This rekindled the debate that PASOK and KKE had led in the deliberations before the proclamation of the 1975 Constitution and polarized the political environment, as it undermined the consensus basis between PASOK and New Democracy that had functioned reasonably well between 1981 and 1985.[2]

Both the choice of Sartzetakis, who had acquired fame exactly due to his struggle against Greece's right-wing "deep state", and the beginning of the constitutional reform process underscored the following: The weakening of the balancing role that the president played against the prime minister and the reinforcement of the majoritarian elements of Greek democracy were the two main aims. On a populist vein, the PASOK government claimed that it would not only shed the last vestiges of a state that was only procedurally democratic, but it also aimed to realize promises about the introduction of a "truly democratic" regime. Pledging on the completion of the transition to democracy, which began in 1974, PASOK argued that the elimination of the executive powers of the president would remove one of the last vestiges of early Cold-war authoritarianism . This became clear in the parliamentary deliberations about the amendment of the constitution. Although the successful cohabitation of Karamanlis and Papandreou between 1981 and 1985 had shown that the balance introduced by the 1975 Constitution was not prone to political crisis, the PASOK administration decided to eliminate what it coined as "presidential superpowers". Anastassios Peponis, the parliamentary rapporteur for PASOK who introduced the constitutional amendment package to the parliamentary plenary, stated in his speech that

> Invoking the lack of use of some provisions, their lack of implementation is by no means an argument to keep them in the current constitution. The question is what is our guiding principle? When provisions directly or indirectly contradict the principle of popular sovereignty, we object to them.

....We support that the president is neither directly appointed by nor elected by the people. We are not a presidential, we are a parliamentary democracy. It is not the president who resorts to the people, so that the people deliver a verdict by majority voting. It is the legitimate government. It is the political parties. If the president resorts to the people, then he inevitably either sides with one party against others or attempts to substitute himself for the parties and impose his own solution. Nevertheless, as soon as he attempts to substitute himself for the parties and impose his own solution, then he embarks upon the formation of his own decisions of governmental nature. Then the government, directly or indirectly, fully or partially, is abolished.[3]

Peponis' arguments were countered by Anna Psarouda-Benaki, the parliamentary rapporteur of the major opposition party, New Democracy. Psarouda-Benaki argued on a completely different line stating that

And this is the achievement of the 1975 Constitution: A miraculous balance between the Parliament, the Government and the President of the Republic, namely these state organs which express popular sovereignty and always pose the risk of de facto usurping it... . It is also interesting to see where these competences of the President of the Republic are transferred. They are removed from him, but where do they go? To popular sovereignty and the Parliament, as the parliamentary majority claims? Dear colleagues, all of them go to the government, either directly or indirectly through the parliamentary majority controlled by it. Because the parliament is now subjugated to the parliamentary majority through party discipline... . Dear colleagues, the conclusion from the amendments suggested by the government or the parliamentary majority is the following: Power is transferred completely to the government. Hence, we have every reason to be afraid and suspect and mistrust about the future of Greece... . I want to stress the following, so that we, the Greek people, understand well: that with the suggested amendments you turn government and government majority into superpowers.[4]

Psarouda-Benaki's speech underscored the threat of majoritarianism for the quality of Greek democracy as well as for social cohesion and stability. Yet her argument could not overturn the sound parliamentary majority that PASOK enjoyed. The parliament endorsed with qualified majority the constitutional amendment package and reapproved it in early 1986, following the comfortable victory of PASOK in the June 1985 parliamentary elections.[5] Greece made a decisive shift towards majoritarianism, and this was not different from developments in other Southern European states.[6] The survey held by Lijphart reinforced the argument about strong majoritarian tendencies in Greece following the 1985–1986 constitutional amendment.[7]

While there was no constitutional amendment between 1986 and 2001, there were occasional statements of strong political figures that pointed towards the reinforcement of majoritarian tendencies. Konstantinos Mitsotakis, a leader of New Democracy and prime minister between 1990 and 1993, advocated throughout his lengthy political career the direct popular election of the president and the restoration of his powers at the expense of the judiciary (see p. 46). Extreme majoritarian ideas were also not unheard of among the Greek centre-left and were often confounded with populism. Andreas Papandreou, the founding president of PASOK and prime minister between 1981 and 1989 and 1993 and 1996, once famously exclaimed in an election rally in Kozani that "there are no institutions, but only the people".[8] While these statements failed to lead to a constitutional reform process in the 1990s, not least because of the rather rigid conditions and the qualified majority required, the Greek constitution would undergo amendments in the first decade of the new millennium.

THE CONSTITUTIONAL AMENDMENTS OF 2001 AND 2008

The second amendment of the 1975 Constitution was held by the centre-left PASOK government of Kostas Simitis in 2001.[9] Setting the "modernization" of Greek politics and society and Greece's membership of the Eurozone as its key objectives, the Simitis administration departed to a large extent from the populist legacy of Andreas Papandreou's PASOK. It attempted to bring the constitution in line with contemporary developments in the fields of human rights and address some of the chronic deficiencies of the Greek political system.[10] A total of 71 amendment proposals were introduced, and in the end 48 articles were amended, a large number considering constitutional amendments in most European countries.[11] While most amendments aimed to introduce or better protect human rights, those which attracted the most attention were those aiming to tackle corruption. Members of parliament were barred from having parallel paid professional activities, while shareholders of media corporations were barred from participating in public procurement tenders.[12] Moreover, the promotion of the institutional independence of the "independent authorities" was a step that certainly reinforced their function as checks-and-balances mechanisms against the power of the executive.

While majoritarian tendencies were not represented in the constitutional amendment text, they were, by no means, absent in the political debates. Some of the original reform proposals, put forward by Evangelos Venizelos a government minister, professor of constitutional law and rapporteur for the incumbent PASOK, involved narrowing the range of cases that could be subject to the review of the Council of State, Greece's supreme administrative court. Other provisions effectively delayed the process of constitutional review. Venizelos expressed in his writings and parliamentary speeches Rousseauian views that tended to downplay the significance of checks and balances and highlight majoritarian definitions of democracy. This became clear in particular when the discussion came to the competences of "independent authorities", which Venizelos refused to recognize as key checks-and-balances mechanisms. In his view:

> [Administrative agencies] do not function, or rather should not function as counter-majoritarian checks and balances, but as guarantees that either relate to the legal or to the democratic and pluralistic character of our constitution, through the protection of the autonomy of politics against the concentration of economic, communicational [sic], and, at the end of the day, political influence. Independent agencies from this point of view function just like judicial power, which is not (should not be) an institutional, that is a political, check on the political institutions of the State, but a guarantor of the democratic rule of law.[13]

In Venizelos' view, independent authorities were additional guarantees for the "democratic rule of law", i.e. the will of the majority, as expressed through the democratic process. This would lead to power centralization against private interests and a state, which allows the majority to play a key role in the definition of political and social values.

These views were rebutted by Nicos C. Alivizatos, a professor of constitutional law and student of Aristovoulos Manessis,[14] who insisted on the importance of independent administrative authorities as a key checks-and-balances mechanism. According to Alivizatos,

under both its parliamentary and the presidential version, modern democracy means that the majority does not rule unchecked. On the contrary it
introduces checks and balances to arrest the action of the rulers, whenever
they take a wrong turn . . . Only after the legal assumption of power by
Mussolini in Italy and Hitler in Germany through elections, did European
legal thought realize that for democracy to survive and for minority interests to be secure, it is necessary that we go beyond the law of the majority.
We need checks; we need guardians of the constitution. In post-war constitutions, this role is played by judges and independent agencies."[15]

In the end, Venizelos' majoritarian-leaning proposals did not prove
appealing. Failing to enjoy the consent of Prime Minister Kostas Simitis,
they were outvoted by deputies of both PASOK and New Democracy at
the later stages of the amendment process.[16]

The second constitutional amendment was held in 2008 by the conservative government of Kostas Karamanlis. 38 amendment proposals
were submitted in 2006. Majoritarian-leaning amendment proposals like
the introduction of the direct election of the president by the people in
case the parliament failed to elect one counterbalanced proposals such
as the establishment of a supreme constitutional court. Given the lack
of collaboration between the government and opposition parties and the
slim parliamentary majority of the government party, the amendment
proved far more limited in scope than the previous one. Only three of
the initial 38 amendment proposals were approved. One of the most
controversial reforms of the 2001 amendment, the prohibition of any
paid professional occupation for the parliamentary deputies was repealed.
The other other two amendments referred to increased parliamentary
rights on amending and monitoring the implementation of state budg-
ets and taking special legislative care for the insular and mountainous
regions of Greece.[17]

THE CONSTITUTIONAL DEBATES OF 2016

The outbreak of the Greek economic crisis in fall 2009 had a catalytic
effect on Greek politics. Successive governments promised and failed to
bring an end to the economic debacle, through the half-hearted implementation of reform programmes which were part and parcel of the
financial package agreements that Greece signed with its creditors, the
European Central Bank (ECB), the European Commission and the

International Monetary Fund (IMF). Under these circumstances, a debate on the amendment of the Greek constitution appeared redundant and did not emerge until 2016.

The advent of the SYRIZA–ANEL coalition government in January 2015 did not appear to promise a fundamental shift in the Greek constitution. Tracing its origins to the radical left but increasingly reminding PASOK of the 1980s the closer it came to power, SYRIZA had engaged in a fiercely populist rhetoric that accused its opponents of "working against the interests of the Greek people". SYRIZA also promised to bring an end to austerity policies that it considered responsible for the plight of Greek economy and society, without making any reference to the constitution. This changed suddenly in summer 2016, when Prime Minister Alexis Tsipras declared his intention to launch a daunting constitutional reform process. Among the proposals submitted, there existed a clear preference for the enhancement of the majoritarian features of Greek democracy. One was the possibility of direct election of the president.[18] According to this suggestion, the president would be elected by the parliament with a qualified majority of two-thirds in two consecutive votes. If these votes prove fruitless, then the people would directly elect one of the first two candidates that emerged from the parliamentary vote. Tsipras also suggested a "within reason" enhancement of the competences of the president "with the aim to reinforce his regulating, stabilizing and guarantor role, without this touching the core of the parliamentary system". Examples included the ability of the president to address the parliament on "important occasions", to call meetings of the "Political Party Leaders Council", consisting of the leaders of the parties represented in parliament, or to refer approved bills to a special consultative body, exclusively consisting of judges, to evaluate their constitutionality.[19]

In addition, and in his expressed aim to "promote direct democracy", Tsipras proposed a series of amendments intended to make referendums a key element of Greek politics. First, he suggested that any treaty transferring sovereign competences of the state would have to be ratified through referendum. Another major innovation was the introduction of referendums by popular initiative. A referendum on a "national issue" could be initiated by 500,000 citizens; one million signatures would suffice for a referendum to reject a bill approved by parliament—with the exception of budgetary bills, or to initiate legislation on any matter. Currently, referendums on "crucial national issues" may only be held following a decision of the absolute majority in parliament. Moreover, Tsipras promised consultation and public debate on the parliamentary control of "independent authorities", such as the Ombudsman office and the Radio-Television Council, as well as on the establishment of new. "Independent authorities" were implicitly considered "bastions of elitism" and obstacles to the expression of *volonté générale*.[20]

What further reinforced the majoritarian underpinnings of the initiative was the announcement of a constitutional consultation process which invited popular participation and supplemented the role of the parliament despite clear constitutional prerogatives. An "Organizing Committee" would be established, with the aim to conduct public debates and consultation at the municipal level with professional associations, chambers of commerce, non-governmental associations and citizens. The output of these deliberations would then be evaluated by regional assemblies. At the end of the process, the 'Organizing Committee' would synthesize the input and submit a report to all political parties, which would then move on with the constitutional amendment procedure.[21]

On the other hand, the constitutional amendment package included suggestions that could reinforce the consensus elements of the Greek democracy. Most importantly, Tsipras suggested constitutionally establishing proportional representation as the Greek electoral system.[22] In addition, following the German example, Tsipras suggested the introduction of "constructive vote of no-confidence". This would mean that the parliament could not vote down a government through a vote of no-confidence, as is now the case, without simultaneously agreeing to vote a successor. Fulfilling a long-standing demand of the Greek left as well as calculations about the dwindling electoral prospects of SYRIZA may have contributed to these deviating steps from majoritarianism.[23]

NOTES

1. On this, see Mavrias, "Οι Αναθεωρήσεις του Συντάγματος του 1975 [The Amendments of the 1975 Constitution]".
2. Voulgaris, *Η Ελλάδα της Μεταπολίτευσης 1974–1990* [*Greece of the Transition 1974–1990*], pp. 260–270.

3. Hellenic Parliament [Βουλή των Ελλήνων], Πρακτικά των Συνεδριάσεων [*Parliamentary Proceedings*] (Athens: Hellenic Parliament [Βουλή των Ελλήνων], 1986), p. 135.

4. Ibid., pp. 138–140.

5. According to Article 110 of the Greek constitution, any constitutional amendment will require the approval of the current parliament and the one after the next elections, by an absolute majority in one and a three-fifth majority of the 300 deputies in the other.

6. For a comparison of Greek majoritarianism with other Southern European cases, see Lijphart et al., "A Mediterranean Model of Democracy? The Southern European Democracies in Comparative Perspective", pp. 20–22.

7. Lijphart, *Patterns of Democracy: Government Forms and Performance in Thirty-Six Countries*, p. 110.

8. Hans-Jürgen Puhle, "Mobilizers and Late Modernizers: Socialist Parties in the New Southern Europe" in P. Nikiforos Diamandouros and Richard Gunther, eds., *Parties, Politics, and Democracy in the New Southern Europe* (Baltimore MD: John Hopkins University Press, 2001), p. 319.

9. Mavrias, "Οι Αναθεωρήσεις του Συντάγματος του 1975 [The Amendments of the 1975 Constitution]".

10. Pavlos Eleftheriadis, "Constitutional Reform and the Rule of Law in Greece", *West European Politics*, Vol. 28, no. 2 (2005), pp. 323–324.

11. Nicos Alivizatos and Pavlos Eleftheriadis, "South European Briefing-the Greek Constitutional Amendments of 2001", *South European Society and Politics*, Vol. 7, no. 1 (2002), pp. 64–65.

12. Both initiatives proved controversial, and results proved largely questionable. While addressing these questions through constitutional provisions and not through regular legislation betrayed some concern about the effectiveness of these steps and hope that raising their institutional weight would improve their applicability, in fact little was achieved. On this, see Nicos C. Alivizatos, *Ο Αβέβαιος Εκσυγχρονισμός και η Θολή Συνταγματική Αναθεώρηση* [*The Uncertain Modernization and the Opaque Constitutional Reform*] (Athens: Πόλις [Polis], 2001).

13. Evangelos Venizelos, Το *Αναθεωρητικό Κεκτημένο: Το Συνταγματικό Φαινόμενο στον 21ο Αιώνα και η Εισφορά της Αναθεώρησης του 2001* [*The Amendment's Achievement: The Constitutional Phenomenon in the 21st Century and the Contribution of the Amendment of 2001*] (Athens: Σάκκουλα [Sakkoula], 2001), p. 227, cited in Eleftheriadis, "Constitutional Reform and the Rule of Law in Greece", p. 330.

14. Aristovoulos Manessis was a professor of constitutional law that left a strong imprint on the 1986 constitutional reform debate with his argument against the reinforcement of majoritarian elements in the Greek constitution.

15. Alivizatos, *O Αβέβαιος Εκσυγχρονισμός και η Θολή Συνταγματική Αναθεώρηση* [*The Uncertain Modernization and the Opaque Constitutional Reform*], p. 223 cited in Eleftheriadis, "Constitutional Reform and the Rule of Law in Greece", p. 329. Also see, Yannis A. Tassopoulos, *Τα Θεσμικά Αντίβαρα της Εξουσίας και η Αναθεώρηση του Συντάγματος* [*Institutional Checks and Balances and Constitutional Amendment*] (Athens & Thessaloniki: Σάκκουλα [Sakkoula], 2007).
16. Alivizatos and Eleftheriadis, "South European Briefing-The Greek Constitutional Amendments of 2001"
17. Hellenic Parliament, *Parliamentary Resolution of 27 May 2008 of the VIII Revisionary Parliament* [*Κοινοβουλευτικό Ψήφισμα της 8ης Αναθεωρητικής Βουλής της 27ης Μαΐου 2008*].
18. The direct election of the President was first introduced in the Greek constitutional debate by Konstantinos Mitsotakis (see p. 46).
19. Ioannis N. Grigoriadis, *The Greece Constitutional Reform Process: Towards Direct Democracy and Secularism?* (International Institute for Democracy & Electoral Assistance (IDEA): Stockholm, 2016), available from http://www.constitutionnet.org/news/greece-constitutional-reform-process-towards-direct-democracy-and-secularism [posted on 24/8/2016].
20. Ibid.
21. Ibid.
22. For a typology of electoral systems, see Pippa Norris, "Choosing Electoral Systems: Proportional, Majoritarian and Mixed Systems", *International Political Science Review*, Vol. 18, no. 3 (1997), pp. 299–306.
23. An electoral system based on proportional representation has been a historic demand of the Greek left since the post-World War II era. Under Greece's current electoral system, the first (winning) political party gets a bonus of up to 50 seats.

REFERENCES

Nicos Alivizatos and Pavlos Eleftheriadis, "South European Briefing-the Greek Constitutional Amendments of 2001", *South European Society and Politics*, Vol. 7, no. 1 (2002), pp. 63–71.
Nicos C. Alivizatos, *O Αβέβαιος Εκσυγχρονισμός και η Θολή Συνταγματική Αναθεώρηση* [*The Uncertain Modernization and the Opaque Constitutional Reform*] (Athens: Πόλις [Polis], 2001).
Pavlos Eleftheriadis, "Constitutional Reform and the Rule of Law in Greece", *West European Politics*, Vol. 28, no. 2 (2005), pp. 317–334.
Ioannis N. Grigoriadis, *The Greece Constitutional Reform Process: Towards Direct Democracy and Secularism?* (International Institute for Democracy &

Electoral Assistance (IDEA): Stockholm, 2016), available from http://www.constitutionnet.org/news/greece-constitutional-reform-process-towards-direct-democracy-and-secularism [posted on 24/8/2016].

Hellenic Parliament, *Parliamentary Resolution of 27 May 2008 of the VIII Revisionary Parliament* [*Κοινοβουλευτικό Ψήφισμα της 8ης Αναθεωρητικής Βουλής της 27ης Μαΐου 2008*] (Athens, 2008).

Hellenic Parliament [Βουλή των Ελλήνων], *Πρακτικά των Συνεδριάσεων* [*Parliamentary Proceedings*] (Athens: Hellenic Parliament [Βουλή των Ελλήνων], 1986).

Arend Lijphart, *Patterns of Democracy: Government Forms and Performance in Thirty-Six Countries* (New Haven, CT: Yale University Press, 1999).

Arend Lijphart, Thomas C. Bruneau, P. Nikiforos Diamandouros and Richard Gunther, "A Mediterranean Model of Democracy? The Southern European Democracies in Comparative Perspective", *West European Politics*, Vol. 11, no. 1 (1988), pp. 7–25.

Kostas Mavrias, "Οι Αναθεωρήσεις του Συντάγματος του 1975 [The Amendments of the 1975 Constitution]" in Hellenic Parliament [Βουλή των Ελλήνων], ed., *30 Χρόνια από το Σύνταγμα του 1975: Τα Ελληνικά Συντάγματα από το Ρήγα Έως Σήμερα* [*30 Years from the 1975 Constitution: Greek Constitutions from Rigas until Today*] (Athens: Hellenic Parliament [Βουλή των Ελλήνων], 2005), pp. 233–266.

Pippa Norris, "Choosing Electoral Systems: Proportional, Majoritarian and Mixed Systems", *International Political Science Review*, Vol. 18, no. 3 (1997), pp. 297–312.

Hans-Jürgen Puhle, "Mobilizers and Late Modernizers: Socialist Parties in the New Southern Europe" in P. Nikiforos Diamandouros and Richard Gunther, eds., *Parties, Politics, and Democracy in the New Southern Europe* (Baltimore MD: John Hopkins University Press, 2001), pp. 268–328.

Yannis A. Tassopoulos, *Τα Θεσμικά Αντίβαρα της Εξουσίας και η Αναθεώρηση του Συντάγματος* [*Institutional Checks and Balances and Constitutional Amendment*] (Athens & Thessaloniki: Σάκκουλα [Sakkoula], 2007).

Evangelos Venizelos, *Το Αναθεωρητικό Κεκτημένο: Το Συνταγματικό Φαινόμενο στον 21ο Αιώνα και η Εισφορά της Αναθεώρησης του 2001* [*The Amendment's Achievement: The Constitutional Phenomenon in the 21st Century and the Contribution of the Amendment of 2001*] (Athens: Σάκκουλα [Sakkoula], 2001).

Yannis Voulgaris, *Η Ελλάδα της Μεταπολίτευσης 1974–1990* [*Greece of the Transition 1974–1990*] (Athens: Θεμέλιο [Themelio], 2001).

CHAPTER 5

The Rising Tide of Populist Majoritarianism in Turkey

Abstract The rising tide of populist majoritarianism in Turkish constitutional debates is indexed to the rise of the AKP into a hegemonic position in Turkish politics. While early constitutional reform deliberations focused on the introduction of a new liberal democratic constitution, following the 2010 constitutional referendum emphasis shifted towards the introduction of a presidential system. The constitutional draft submitted to the parliament in January 2017 and to a referendum in April 2017 boosted majoritarian elements to an unprecedented degree.

Keywords AKP · Erdoğan · Presidentialism · Referendum Turkey · Majoritarianism · Amendment

THE RISE OF THE AKP

The gradual consolidation of the AKP rule emerged as a key permissive condition for the re-emergence of majoritarian debates in Turkey. The constitutional referendum that took place in 2010 failed to address all the necessary changes, and a discussion about the drafting of a brand new constitution from scratch emerged. While this was a ripe request given the incompatibility of the 1982 Constitution with a liberal democratic regime, the constitutional debate eventually shifted away from its original agenda. Instead of the introduction of an effective liberal democratic constitution, one started discussing the introduction of a presidential system,

© The Author(s) 2018   53
I.N. Grigoriadis, *Democratic Transition and the Rise of Populist Majoritarianism*, Reform and Transition in the Mediterranean,
DOI 10.1007/978-3-319-57556-8_5

boosting majoritarianism and weakening checks-and-balances mechanisms. Such a constitutional draft was submitted in January 2017 to the Turkish parliament and was put to a referendum on 16 April 2017, collecting the approval of 51.4 percent of the Turkish voters.

Populism was, by no means, a novelty in Turkish politics. Ever since the advent of multiparty politics in 1946, religious conservative political parties have employed a discourse dividing Turkish society between "oppressing secularist elites" and the "oppressed pious people". Coming from the "periphery" of Turkish politics, they challenged the hegemonic position of Kemalist "centre".[1] This was put in even more assertive terms within the realm of Turkish political Islam under Necmettin Erbakan and Recep Tayyip Erdoğan: Secularists were called "white Turks (*beyaz Türkler*)", while religious conservatives were "black Turks (*siyah*

Fig. 5.1 The 2013 Gezi protests comprised a rare collaboration opportunity for secularist and conservative opposition groups: The tent of the "Revolutionary Muslims (Devrimci Müslümanlar)"

Türkler)" who had suffered under the rule of "white Turk" elites since the late years of the Ottoman Empire and whose only genuine political representative was Islamist political parties. "White Turks" were members of an elite that had been alienated from the people and hence could stand for its true interests. On the other hand, "black Turks" were the true, "oppressed" Turkish people. The AKP made use of this rhetoric on its way to power, but did not give it up even after 2002 when "secularist elites" ceased to rule the country. The new discourse pointed at the control of the military, bureaucracy and the judiciary by the "white Turks". As the AKP was consolidating step by step its power through consecutive electoral victories, confidant appointments in the state apparatus, issues regarding the public manifestation of Islam became instrumental in maintaining the polarization between secularists and pious conservatives. This was also achieved through an onslaught against dissident NGOs and the support of subservient civil society organizations.[2] The rhetorical distinction between "old Turkey", run by "corrupt", "un-national" elites and "new Turkey", governed by the AKP as the true representative of the *volonté générale* and the people, served similar objectives (Fig. 5.1).[3]

CONSTITUTIONAL AMENDMENTS OF 2007–2010

The constitution and its content had become one of the focal contention points between the AKP and the secularist elites of the country, since the rise of the AKP to power in November 2002. Many secularists harboured severe doubts regarding the sincerity of AKP intentions and appeared unwilling to cede the tutelary role circumscribed by the 1982 constitution. President Ahmet Necdet Sezer acted in his balancing capacity by vetoing numerous government bills throughout his "cohabitation" with the AKP government between 2002 and 2007.[4] When his tenure ended, a major constitutional crisis erupted when the military and the judiciary objected to the candidacy of Foreign Minister Abdullah Gül for president, because his wife wore a headscarf.[5] The army's general staff issued an electronic memorandum on 27 April 2007 in which it clearly took position against the candidacy of Gül. Gül's candidacy also faced additional obstacles, when the Constitutional Court issued a surprise decision raising the quorum of the presidential election, thus rendering impossible the otherwise easy election of Gül. Following the constitutional deadlock, the government called for early elections and introduced a constitutional amendment bill calling—among others—for the direct election of the president and a brand new, "civilian" constitution. This met with the reaction of President Sezer, who referred it back to the parliament, stating that changing the method of electing the president was not just a "procedural" modification but also one directly touching upon the core of the political system. Sezer argued that a popularly elected president could dominate the political system and cause friction and conflict within the executive. His argument did not convince the parliament, which adopted the amendment bill *verbatim*.[6]

The parliamentary elections of 22 June 2007 led to a resounding victory for the AKP with 46.6% of the vote, which underlined popular support for its political programme. The constitutional amendment was completed by the new parliament. Remaining questions, such as the direct election of the president by the people and the reduction of his tenure from 7 to 5 years, were endorsed by referendum on 21 October 2007. Yet this was not the last episode in the conflict between the AKP government and the bureaucracy. Following a government initiative for lifting the ban on the headscarf in universities through a constitutional amendment, a closure case was filed in March 2008 against the AKP at the Constitutional Court by the Chief Prosecutor Abdurrahman Yalçınkaya. Yalçınkaya argued that the AKP had become a "focal point" of anti-secular activities and requested its closure. The Constitutional Court annulled the amendment in June 2008, due to its alleged incompatibility with the principle of secularism, but fell short of banning the AKP with its verdict of 30 July 2008. Following this ruling, the AKP pushed towards a new constitutional amendment bill, which—among others—enabled the prosecution of the 1980 coup leaders, introduced the institution of Ombudsman and modified the rules of appointing the senior members of the judiciary, by means of increasing parliamentary and government control. This bill was approved by popular referendum on 12 September 2010.

Meanwhile, a series of criminal investigations, including *Ergenekon*, *Balyoz* and *Andıç*, were launched to investigate alleged "deep state" and military coup plots against the AKP administration following its rise to power in 2002. In the framework of these, scores of active and retired officers, including two former Chiefs of General Staff, were arrested and detained. This signalled a decisive shift in the direction of civilianization of Turkish politics and the diminution of the political influence of the military. It also raised severe concerns about the rule of law as far as the

Fig. 5.2 A campaign poster of the AKP supporting the "Yes" vote in the 12 September 2010 constitutional referendum

conduct of these investigations and trials was concerned and whether victims and oppressors were shifting sides (Fig. 5.2).

The first signs of a shift towards majoritarianism became evident in the constitutional amendments introduced by the AKP in 2007 and 2010. The popular election of the president was followed by steps, which limited the institutional autonomy of the judiciary, the military and civil bureaucracy. In the face of what had transpired in 2007 and 2008, this move looked legitimate. The military and the judiciary had appeared unwilling to allow the consolidation of the AKP power; yet their balancing influence was not always exercised within the limits of the democratic government and the rule of law. The way of their intervention in crucial constitutional and political processes had disclosed that their interest lay not in the protection of the democratic regime, but rather of their tutelary role and privileges. The spectre of *juristocracy* or military tutelage over government facilitated the alignment of democratic forces on the side of the AKP government and helped secure comfortable parliamentary majorities in the parliamentary elections of 2007 and 2011, as well as a clear positive vote in the 2010 constitutional referendum. Yet, while the AKP administration had rendered crucial services to the cause of democratic consolidation in Turkey in its first term, its commitment to the goal started waning towards the end of the 2000s.[7] Rising concerns about a resurgence of authoritarian tendencies were recorded by domestic and international NGOs.[8] In addition, the risk of political deadlock in the case of conflicting views between the president and the government was also underlined (Fig. 5.3).[9]

The AKP Initiative to Introduce a Presidential System

The weakening of existing undemocratic checks and balances against the government became a permissive condition for the strengthening of majoritarian views within the ranks of the government party. The 2007 amendment of the constitution that introduced the direct election of the president by the people was a first step towards the reinforcement of presidential powers and a shift towards majoritarianism. While the direct election of the president was not tantamount with an increase of his powers, it definitely increased his popular legitimacy and reduced his political dependence on the legislative. As his legitimacy was no more derived from the parliament through his indirect election, the powers of the president against the prime minister and the legislative could now be

Fig. 5.3 A campaign poster of four small left-wing parties inviting to a "Hayır (No)" demonstration before the 12 September 2010 constitutional referendum

strengthened. The popular election of the president appeared to be the first step towards a reconfiguration of the balance of power between the executive, the judiciary and the legislative, as well as within the executive, between the president, the government and the bureaucracy.

This trend was amplified by the rise of the AKP to a hegemonic position in Turkish politics. Following three consecutive electoral victories in 2002, 2007 and 2011 with rising popular appeal and given Turkey's profound socioeconomic changes,[10] it was debated whether Turkey was leaving multipartyism and *de facto* entering a dominant party system.[11] Soon the debate about Turkey's new constitution shifted from the aim of achieving Turkey's democratic consolidation to that of introducing a robust presidential system, which could complete the shift towards a purely majoritarian regime. This shift was linked with the expressed ambitions of Prime Minister Recep Tayyip Erdoğan. Following three terms as prime minister, Erdoğan repeatedly underlined his preference

for the introduction of a presidential system[12] and declared his ambi-
tion to become Turkey's first directly elected president. Discussions
about the weaknesses of the parliamentary system and the strengths
of the French semi-presidential[13] or the American presidential system
proliferated in mass media. These reinforced majoritarian views within
Turkey's government party, which soon found expression in its constitutional amendment proposals. The presidential system was presented as a
panacea for all Turkey's constitutional and government problems. Party
officials charged the parliamentary system with lack of transparency, corruption, inefficiency, instability and proneness to consecutive crises.[14] In
contrast to that, the introduction of a solid presidential system would
allow Turkey "to move fast forward on the path of progress and development." In a booklet published by the government party to promote the
presidential system, it was stated that:

> ....Turkish democracy suffered heavy wounds because of the instability
> caused by economic and social crises....The democratization steps of the
> AKP became possible thanks to its single-party governments. Nevertheless,
> it may not be possible that our parliamentary system always produces
> strong single party governments. For that reason, it will be in the long
> term to the benefit of our country to introduce a change in the govern-
> ment system of Turkey....The parliamentary system has clearly proven to
> be unsuitable to Turkey's needs and the requirements of the time....The
> solution is the presidential system, which creates stability in democracy and
> secures fast, effective and healthy decision making.....Because Turkey has
> no time to lose and no energy to waste to reach its 2023 objectives. In the
> process of globalization, it is only with the transition to the presidential
> system that the country's government can make quick, influential and pro-
> ductive decisions.[15]

Debates in the parliamentary committee with the duty to work on the
amendment of the constitution highlighted a shift in the position of the
government party. While in the early phases of the debate the French
semi-presidential or the US presidential model was used as sources of
inspiration, in the parliamentary debates a different presidential model
was put forward. According to the constitutional draft submitted by the
AKP in early 2013, the president would acquire substantially more powers than his French or US counterpart, which would include the power
to dissolve the parliament. The Deputy Prime Minister Bekir Bozdağ
and the head of the parliamentary committee on the constitution Burhan

Kuzu reportedly pitied US President Barack Obama for his inability to pass a series of critical bills, or even decide on issues as menial as the appointment of a US ambassador without the consent of the Congress.[16] What "poor Obama" suffered, the Turkish president should not. What emerged as the AKP proposal was a "super-presidential" model, in which the president would enjoy key additional powers to those normally awarded to presidents in presidential systems. According to the draft, the president would enjoy:

a. the power to dissolve the parliament at his own discretion and
b. the power to issue administrative decrees, regardless of the consent of the government and the parliament.[17]

Both suggested powers implied that a new "Turkish-style" presidential model was in the making, which would secure vast powers to the president. These would be reminiscent of the powers awarded in some "super-presidential" systems in Latin America of the 1980s, also known with the term "*decretismo*".[18]

Against these proposals, the opposition charged the government with the aim to establish an authoritarian regime. Concerns about the possible degeneration of Turkish democracy were in resonance with the views of several experts. The "zero-sum game" approach, which the presidential system was conducive to, was feared to incite social polarization at a time Turkey has already been suffering by deep social and ethnic divisions.[19] The incompatibility of Turkish political culture with a strong presidential system, the low level of social trust and risk of power accumulation[20] and the personalistic character of Turkish politics,[21] as well as the risk of fomenting authoritarianism and instability,[22] had already been raised in the academic literature, long before the debate about Turkey's government system captured public attention.[23] Despite these concerns, it seemed likely that the AKP constitutional amendment bill could garner a qualified majority of three-fifths and be submitted to a referendum. Concerns about the reversal of Turkey's democratization process became more explicit during the Gezi events of May–June 2013 and following the AKP government reaction against the 17–25 December 2013 graft investigation (Fig. 5.4).

As Prime Minister Erdoğan became the first directly elected president in the presidential elections of 10 August 2014, he wished to maintain influence on day-to-day politics despite the fact that the constitution

Fig. 5.4   A "List of Commandments" from the 2013 Gezi Protest Camp

bestowed the bulk of executive powers upon the prime minister. His appointment of Ahmet Davutoğlu as prime minister was meant to serve that aim, as Davutoğlu was known as a low-profile politician who would presumably not challenge Erdoğan's micromanagement ambitions. The president acquired an increasingly influential position in the state apparatus, and the resolution of critical political issues such as the Kurdish issue became less institutionalized and more linked to his personal initiatives. These once again underscored the strengths as well as the perils of presidentialism in the context of seeking a peaceful solution to the long-standing Kurdish question.[24] Many on both sides of the Kurdish conflict hoped that a strong Erdoğan would be the only person able to reach the compromises necessary for a fair and lasting solution of the Kurdish question. Nonetheless, following the parliamentary election of 1 June 2015 that left AKP for the first time since its foundation short of a parliamentary majority and a series of terrorist attacks, the Turkish president decided to abandon the "peace process" aiming to resolve Turkey's Kurdish question. War resumed, and in the new parliamentary elections of November 2015, the AKP won a comfortable parliamentary majority.[25] While the hegemony of the AKP and indispensable role of President Erdoğan were reconfirmed, the Kurdish question was heading into a new vicious circle of violence.

THE CONSTITUTIONAL DEBATES OF 2016-THE APRIL 2017 REFERENDUM

The constitutional reform debate took a critical turn in 2016 in light of the dramatic events of the year. The resignation of Prime Minister Ahmet Davutoğlu and his replacement by Binali Yıldırım in May 2016 was meant to facilitate Erdoğan's plans for the introduction of a presidential system. While Davutoğlu had distanced himself from key aspects of the constitutional amendment espoused by President Erdoğan and his willingness to exercise the prime minister prerogatives recognized by the Turkish constitution, Yıldırım was expected to be loyal to the tactics and the strategic priorities of the Turkish president.

While constitutional reform was high in the government agenda since the rise of Yıldırım to the office of the prime minister, the debate took a radical shift following the abortive coup of 15 July 2016. The promulgation of a state of emergency on 20 July 2016 gave the executive extraordinary powers meant to eradicate all elements of the Gülen movement in

Fig. 5.5 An AKP banner on the April 2017 referendum featuring Prime Minister Yıldırım endorsing the "Yes" vote

the Turkish state who were considered responsible for the failed coup and prevent a new attempt. Tens of thousands of Turkish officers and bureaucrats were fired, detained or arrested, while the purge soon grew beyond any proportion to include government dissidents. Under these extraordinary circumstances, the discussion about the introduction of the presidential system acquired new relevance: "A strong president was necessary to bring Turkey out of the current crisis". The AKP sought and sealed a partnership with the far-right Nationalist Action Party (*Milliyetçi Hareket Partisi*-MHP) to prepare a joint constitutional amendment proposal.[26] The 21-article bill[27] was submitted on 10 December 2016, aiming to introduce presidentialism into the Turkish political system.[28] As the bill collected in January 2017 more than 330 votes or three-fifths of the total number of deputies, a constitutional referendum was set on 16 April 2017 (Fig. 5.5).

Among the most important innovations of the bill was the abolition of the office of the prime minister.[29] All the powers of the executive would be fused into the office of the president. The president would be directly elected for a period of five years and would have the power to issue decrees on issues related to executive power without seeking the consent of the parliament. However, basic rights, personal rights and duties and political rights and duties could not be regulated by presidential decree. In addition, presidential decrees could not address issues regulated by law according to the constitution and clearly set within the law.

Another major new prerogative for the president would be the authority to declare a state of emergency, hitherto belonging to the cabinet. On that occasion, the president would also have the right to rule the country through presidential decrees. At the request of the president, the parliament might decide to extend the period for four months at most. In the event of war, the four-month time limit would not be applicable.[30]

An additional key prerogative for the president would be his ability to restructure all ministries and public institutions. The authorities and responsibilities of the public institutions and organizations within the scope of the central administration, as well as the appointment principles of senior civil servants, would be regulated by presidential decree. This would give the president the ability to have direct power over all levels of the bureaucracy including higher education institutions and foundations.[31]

One of the most extraordinary innovations of the bill was the abolition of the non-partisan character of the presidential office. According to the new constitutional draft, the president wound no more have to be above party politics. In fact, he could remain a political party leader, while being the head of state and the executive. There would be maximum two-term tenure for the president; however, if the president made a call for early parliamentary elections during his or second term, he would be able to seek re-election for a third time.[32]

The proposed bill also suggested a radical overhaul of the power distribution between the president and the parliament. His extensive executive powers would not be balanced by the parliament, the judiciary or another state institution. Vice presidents and ministers would be appointed by the president and would refer to him, without a veto or confirmation right by the parliament. The president would also have the right to dissolve the parliament and call for new elections, effectively ending also his own term. On the other hand, the parliament would not have the right to vote down the president and would only be able to call for early general elections with a qualified majority of 60%.[33]

Moreover, the number of parliamentary deputies would rise from 550 to 600, while the age requirement for deputy selection will be reduced from 25 to 18 years of age. Party candidates who failed to be elected in parliamentary elections would serve as substitute deputies in case a deputy's seat from their respective electoral region becomes vacant.[34]

Regarding presidential immunity, the draft referred the issue to the Constitutional Court through a three-step process. If an absolute majority of the deputies agreed (301 out of 600 deputies), a charge against the president could be brought before the parliament. The president could be referred to a parliamentary investigative commission if 360 out of 600 deputies agree. Following the inquiry made by the commission, a two-thirds majority (400 out of 600 deputies) in a secret ballot would be sought to refer the president to the Supreme Court.[35]

A critical reform affecting the separation of powers and the ability of the judiciary to balance executive power referred to the formation of key judiciary bodies, giving key powers to the president. The structure of the Supreme Board of Judges and Prosecutors (*Hâkimler ve Savcılar Yüksek Kurulu*-HSYK) would be changed and its size would fall from 22 to 12 members, while the chair of the board would remain the justice minister. The president would appoint five members of the board directly, while two members would be elected by the parliament, three members by the Court of Cassation (*Yargıtay*) and one by the Council of State (*Danıştay*). A 60% majority (360 out of 600 deputies) would be sought in the first two rounds of HSYK member election in parliament. If the election remained to the last round, members will be determined through a draw. The number of members of the Constitutional Court would be decreased from 17 to 15, as two members from the to-be-abolished Military Supreme Court of Appeals would be removed. The membership of the National Security Council (*Milli Güvenlik Kurulu*-MGK) would also be amended following the removal of the commander of the Gendarmerie.[36]

According to the set timetable, there would be a transition period until 3 November 2019 or the date of early joint presidential and parliamentary elections. While President Erdoğan would be allowed to restore ties with his party, he would not enjoy the power to issue presidential decrees. In contrast, the reduction of the number of the members of the HSYK and the Constitutional Court, the abolition of the military judicial institutions and the reduction of the election age to 18 years would go into effect before 2019.[37] Local elections would be held in March 2019 and presidential and parliamentary elections would be simultaneously held on 3 November 2019 at the latest.[38] Many constitutional experts saw in constitutional draft not just a decisive shift towards majoritarianism in Turkey. The expected influence of the constitutional reform on the check-and-balance mechanisms of the Turkish political system, combined with the effects of the state of emergency, led many experts to fear that the foundations of Turkish liberal democracy were shaking. Fears about Turkey's drift towards a competitive authoritarian model were mounting. The approval -albeit with a thin majority- of the constitutional draft at the 16 April 2017 referendum only reinforced these concerns.

Notes

1. On this, see Şerif Mardin, "Center-Periphery Relations: A Key to Turkish Politics?", *Daedalus*, Vol. 102, no. 1 (1973), pp. 179–186.
2. Bilge Yabanci, "Populism as the Problem Child of Democracy: The AKP's Enduring Appeal and the Use of Meso-Level Actors", *Southeast European and Black Sea Studies*, Vol. 16, no. 4 (2016), pp. 600–609.
3. Orçun Selçuk, "Strong Presidents and Weak Institutions: Populism in Turkey, Venezuela and Ecuador", *Southeast European and Black Sea Studies*, Vol. 16, no. 4 (2016), pp. 577–578.
4. On the question of the veto power of the Turkish President, see Barış Bahçeci, *Karşılaştırmalı Hukukta ve Türkiye'de Devlet Başkanının Veto Yetkisi* (Ankara: Yetkin, 2008).
5. On this, see Ergun Özbudun, *Türkiye'nin Anayasa Krizi* (Ankara: Liberte, 2009) and Peri Uran, "Turkey's Hasty Constitutional Amendment Devoid of Rational Basis: From a Political Crisis to a Governmental System Change", *Journal of Politics and Law*, Vol. 3, no. 1 (2010), pp. 2–3.
6. Ergun Özbudun and Ömer Faruk Gençkaya, *Democratization and the Politics of Constitution-Making in Turkey* (Budapest & New York: Central European University Press, 2009), pp. 99–100.
7. On the critical question of democratization and the role of the AKP, see the works of William M. Hale and Ergun Özbudun, *Islamism, Democracy and Liberalism in Turkey: The Case of the AKP* (Abingdon; New York: Routledge, 2010), E. Fuat Keyman, "Modernization, Globalization and Democratization in Turkey: The AKP Experience and its Limits", *Constellations*, Vol. 17, no. 2 (2010) and Ziya Onis, "Conservative Globalism at the Crossroads: The Justice and Development Party and the Thorny Path to Democratic Consolidation in Turkey", *Mediterranean Politics*, Vol. 14, no. 1 (2009).

8. Cengiz Çağla, "Turkish Politics: Raison D'état Versus Republic", *International Review of Sociology/Revue Internationale de Sociologie*, Vol. 22, no. 3 (2012), pp. 568–570.

9. Levent Gönenç, "Hükümet Sistemi Tartışmalarında Başkanlı Parlamenter Hükümet Sistemi Seçeneği", *Güncel Hukuk*, Vol. 44 (2007), pp. 39–43.

10. On this, see Ali Çarkoğlu and Ersin Kalaycıoğlu, *The Rising Tide of Conservatism in Turkey*, 1st ed. (New York: Palgrave Macmillan, 2009), pp. 27–64.

11. See Meltem Müftüler-Baç and E. Fuat Keyman, "The Era of Dominant-Party Politics", *Journal of Democracy*, Vol. 23, no. 1 (2012), pp. 91–94, Ali Çarkoğlu, "Turkey's 2011 General Elections: Towards a Dominant Party System?", *Insight Turkey*, Vol. 13, no. 3 (2011) and Canan Aslan-Akman, "The 2011 Parliamentary Elections in Turkey and Challenges Ahead for Democratic Reform under a Dominant Party System", *Mediterranean Politics*, Vol. 17, no. 1 (2012), pp. 79–80.

12. İstanbul Bürosu, "Erdoğan: Gönlümde Başkanlık Sistemi Var", *Sabah*, 6/6/2011.

13. For a study of the French model, see Maurice Duverger, "A New Political System Model: Semi-Presidential Government", *European Journal of Political Research*, Vol. 8, no. 2 (1980). For comparative studies of semi-presidential systems, see Matthew S. Shugart, "Semi-Presidential Systems: Dual Executive and Mixed Authority Patterns", *French Politics*, Vol. 3, no. 3 (2005), Robert Elgie, "A Fresh Look at Semi-Presidentialism Varieties on a Theme", *Journal of Democracy*, Vol. 16, no. 3 (2005) and Robert Elgie, ed., *Semi-Presidentialism in Europe* (Oxford: Oxford University Press, 1999).

14. See, for example, Ömer Faruk Ertürk, "Winner Pays It All: Who Is Loser Then? The Current Parliamentarism in Search of Presidentialism in Turkey", *Turkish Journal of Politics*, Vol. 2, no. 1 (2011) and Recep Türk, "Feasibility of Presidential System in Turkey", *Turkish Journal of Politics*, Vol. 2, no. 1 (2011).

15. AK Parti, *Türkiye Başkanlık Sistemini Konuşuyor* (Ankara: AR-GE Başkanlığı, 2013), pp. 2–3.

16. Mehmet Tezkan, "Obama'nın Zavallı Halı", *Milliyet*, 12/3/2013.

17. Ergun Özbudun, "Başkanlığın Kürtlere Yararı Yok", *Interview with Neşe Düzel, Taraf*, 18/03/2013.

18. On this, see Erdal Onar, "Türkiye'nin Başkanlık Veya Yarı-Başkanlık Sistemine Geçmesi Düşünülmeli Midir?" in Teoman Ergül, ed., *Başkanlık Sistemi* (Ankara: Türkiye Barolar Birliği, 2005), pp. 99–100 and Ergun Özbudun, "Hükûmet Sistemi Tartışmaları (2)", *Zaman*, 9/4/2013.

19. On this, see Serap Yazıcı, *Başkanlık ve Yarı-Başkanlık Sistemleri: Türkiye İçin Bir Değerlendirme [Presidential and Semi-Presidential Systems: An Assessment for Turkey]* (İstanbul: İstanbul Bilgi Üniversitesi Yayınları, 2002), Serap Yazıcı, "Başkanlık Sistemleri: Bir Değerlendirme" in Teoman Ergül, ed., *Başkanlık Sistemi* (Ankara: Türkiye Barolar Birliği, 2005) and Uran, "Turkey's Hasty Constitutional Amendment Devoid of Rational Basis: From a Political Crisis to a Governmental System Change", p. 5.
20. İlter Turan, "Başkanlık Sistemi Sevdası: Zayıf Temelli Bir Özle" in Teoman Ergül, ed., *Başkanlık Sistemi* (Ankara: Türkiye Barolar Birliği, 2005), pp. 117–124.
21. Ergun Özbudun, "Başkanlık Sistemi Tartışmaları" in Teoman Ergül, ed., *Başkanlık Sistemi* (Ankara: Türkiye Barolar Birliği, 2005), p. 111.
22. Ersin Kalaycıoğlu, "Başkanlık Rejimi: Türkiye'nin Diktatörlük Tehdidiyle Sınavı" in Teoman Ergül, ed., *Başkanlık Sistemi* (Ankara: Türkiye Barolar Birliği, 2005), pp. 26–27.
23. Özbudun, "Başkanlık Sistemi Tartışmaları", p. 111.
24. On these, also see Ergun Özbudun, "Hükûmet Sistemi Tartışmaları (1)", *Zaman*, 8/4/2013, Özbudun, "Hükûmet Sistemi Tartışmaları (2)" and Özbudun, "Başkanlığın Kürtlere Yararı Yok".
25. Ziya Öniş, "Turkey's Two Elections: The AKP Comes Back", *Journal of Democracy*, Vol. 27, no. 2 (2016), pp. 150–151.
26. According to Article 175 of the Turkish Constitution, constitutional amendments are approved if they are voted for by two thirds or 367 of the total 550 deputies. If they are voted by three fifths, or 330 of the 550 deputies, their fate is decided by a constitutional referendum.
27. Türkiye Büyük Millet Meclisi (TBMM), *Türkiye Cumhuriyeti Anayasasında Değişiklik Yapılmasına Dair Kanun Teklifi* (2/1504/2016).
28. Ankara Office, "AKP, MHP Take Major Step for System Change", *Hürriyet Daily News*, 10/12/2016, Ali Ünal, "Constitutional Reform to Step up Turkey's Democratization Process", *Daily Sabah*, 11/12/2016.
29. Ibid.
30. *Türkiye Büyük Millet Meclisi (TBMM), Türkiye Cumhuriyeti Anayasasında Değişiklik Yapılmasına Dair Kanun Teklifi.*
31. Ankara Office, "AKP, MHP Take Major Step for System Change".
32. *Türkiye Büyük Millet Meclisi (TBMM), Türkiye Cumhuriyeti Anayasasında Değişiklik Yapılmasına Dair Kanun Teklifi.*
33. Ibid.
34. This provision was removed during the deliberations of the parliamentary committee.

35. *Türkiye Büyük Millet Meclisi (TBMM), Türkiye Cumhuriyeti Anayasasında Değişiklik Yapılmasına Dair Kanun Teklifi.*
36. Ankara Office, "AKP, MHP Take Major Step for System Change".
37. *Türkiye Büyük Millet Meclisi (TBMM), Türkiye Cumhuriyeti Anayasasında Değişiklik Yapılmasına Dair Kanun Teklifi.*
38. Ankara Office, "AKP, MHP Take Major Step for System Change".

References

Canan Aslan-Akman, "The 2011 Parliamentary Elections in Turkey and Challenges Ahead for Democratic Reform under a Dominant Party System", *Mediterranean Politics*, Vol. 17, no. 1 (2012), pp. 77–95.

Barış Bahçeci, *Karşılaştırmalı Hukukta ve Türkiye'de Devlet Başkanının Veto Yetkisi* (Ankara: Yetkin, 2008).

İstanbul Bürosu, "Erdoğan: Gönlümde Başkanlık Sistemi Var", *Sabah*, 6/6/2011.

Cengiz Çağla, "Turkish Politics: Raison D'état Versus Republic", *International Review of Sociology/Revue Internationale de Sociologie*, Vol. 22, no. 3 (2012), pp. 565–574.

Ali Çarkoğlu, "Turkey's 2011 General Elections: Towards a Dominant Party System?", *Insight Turkey*, Vol. 13, no. 3 (2011), pp. 43–62.

Ali Çarkoğlu and Ersin Kalaycıoğlu, *The Rising Tide of Conservatism in Turkey*, 1st ed. (New York: Palgrave Macmillan, 2009).

Maurice Duverger, "A New Political System Model: Semi-Presidential Government", *European Journal of Political Research*, Vol. 8, no. 2 (1980), pp. 165–264.

Robert Elgie, "A Fresh Look at Semi-Presidentialism Varieties on a Theme", *Journal of Democracy*, Vol. 16, no. 3 (2005), pp. 98–112.

Robert Elgie, ed., *Semi-Presidentialism in Europe* (Oxford: Oxford University Press, 1999).

Ömer Faruk Ertürk, "Winner Pays It All: Who Is Loser Then? The Current Parliamentarism in Search of Presidentialism in Turkey", *Turkish Journal of Politics*, Vol. 2, no. 1 (2011), pp. 75–90.

Levent Gönenç, "Hükümet Sistemi Tartışmalarında Başkanlı Parlamenter Hükümet Sistemi Seçeneği", *Güncel Hukuk*, Vol. 44 (2007), pp. 39–43.

William M. Hale and Ergun Özbudun, *Islamism, Democracy and Liberalism in Turkey: The Case of the AKP* (Abingdon; New York: Routledge, 2010).

Ersin Kalaycıoğlu, "Başkanlık Rejimi: Türkiye'nin Diktatörlük Tehdidiyle Sınavı" in Teoman Ergül, ed., *Başkanlık Sistemi* (Ankara: Türkiye Barolar Birliği, 2005), pp. 13–30.

E. Fuat Keyman, "Modernization, Globalization and Democratization in Turkey: The AKP Experience and its Limits", *Constellations*, Vol. 17, no. 2 (2010), pp. 312–327.

Şerif Mardin, "Center-Periphery Relations: A Key to Turkish Politics?", *Daedalus*, Vol. 102, no. 1 (1973), pp. 169–190.

Meltem Müftüler-Baç and 2012E. Fuat Keyman, "The Era of Dominant-Party Politics", *Journal of Democracy*, Vol. 23, no. 1 (2012), pp. 85–99.

Ankara Office, "AKP, MHP Take Major Step for System Change", *Hürriyet Daily News*, 10/12/2016.

Erdal Onar, "Türkiye'nin Başkanlık Veya Yarı-Başkanlık Sistemine Geçmesi Düşünülmeli Midir?" in Teoman Ergül, ed., *Başkanlık Sistemi* (Ankara: Türkiye Barolar Birliği, 2005), pp. 71–104.

Ziya Öniş, "Conservative Globalism at the Crossroads: The Justice and Development Party and the Thorny Path to Democratic Consolidation in Turkey", *Mediterranean Politics*, Vol. 14, no. 1 (2009), pp. 21–40.

Ziya Öniş, "Turkey's Two Elections: The AKP Comes Back", *Journal of Democracy*, Vol. 27, no. 2 (2016), pp. 141–154.

Ergun Özbudun, "Başkanlığın Kürtlere Yararı Yok", *Interview with Neşe Düzel, Taraf*, 18/03/2013.

Ergun Özbudun, "Başkanlık Sistemi Tartışmaları" in Teoman Ergül, ed., *Başkanlık Sistemi* (Ankara: Türkiye Barolar Birliği, 2005), pp. 104–112.

Ergun Özbudun, "Hükûmet Sistemi Tartışmaları (1)", *Zaman*, 8/4/2013.

Ergun Özbudun, "Hükûmet Sistemi Tartışmaları (2)", *Zaman*, 9/4/2013.

Ergun Özbudun, *Türkiye'nin Anayasa Krizi* (Ankara: Liberte, 2009).

Ergun Özbudun and Ömer Faruk Gençkaya, *Democratization and the Politics of Constitution-Making in Turkey* (Budapest and New York: Central European University Press, 2009).

AK Parti, *Türkiye Başkanlık Sistemini Konuşuyor* (Ankara: AR-GE Başkanlığı, 2013).

Orçun Selçuk, "Strong Presidents and Weak Institutions: Populism in Turkey, Venezuela and Ecuador", *Southeast European and Black Sea Studies*, Vol. 16, no. 4 (2016), pp. 571–589.

Matthew S. Shugart, "Semi-Presidential Systems: Dual Executive and Mixed Authority Patterns", *French Politics*, Vol. 3, no. 3 (2005), pp. 323–351.

Mehmet Tezkan, "Obama'nın Zavallı Halı", *Milliyet*, 12/3/2013.

İlter Turan, "Başkanlık Sistemi Sevdası: Zayıf Temelli Bir Özle" in Teoman Ergül, ed., *Başkanlık Sistemi* (Ankara: Türkiye Barolar Birliği, 2005), pp. 113–124.

Recep Türk, "Feasibility of Presidential System in Turkey", *Turkish Journal of Politics*, Vol. 2, no. 1 (2011), pp. 33–50.

Türkiye Büyük Millet Meclisi (TBMM), *Türkiye Cumhuriyeti Anayasasında Değişiklik Yapılmasına Dair Kanun Teklifi* (2/1504/2016).

Ali Ünal, "Constitutional Reform to Step up Turkey's Democratization Process", *Daily Sabah*, 11/12/2016.

Peri Uran, "Turkey's Hasty Constitutional Amendment Devoid of Rational Basis: From a Political Crisis to a Governmental System Change", *Journal of Politics and Law*, Vol. 3, no. 1 (2010), pp. 2–10.

Bilge Yabanci, "Populism as the Problem Child of Democracy: The Akp's Enduring Appeal and the Use of Meso-Level Actors", *Southeast European and Black Sea Studies*, Vol. 16, no. 4 (2016), pp. 591–617.

Serap Yazıcı, "Başkanlık Sistemleri: Bir Değerlendirme" in Teoman Ergül, ed., *Başkanlık Sistemi* (Ankara: Türkiye Barolar Birliği, 2005), pp. 125–144.

Serap Yazıcı, Başkanlık ve Yarı-Başkanlık Sistemleri: Türkiye İçin Bir Değerlendirme [Presidential and Semi-Presidential Systems: An Assessment for Turkey] (İstanbul: İstanbul Bilgi Üniversitesi Yayınları, 2002).

CHAPTER 6

Majoritarianism and State Performance

Abstract An evaluation of the reinforcement of majoritarian elements in Greek and Turkish democracy confirms its negative impact on the quality of democratic institutions, transparency and accountability. Boosted by populist politics, it has also nurtured social polarization and prevented the development of social trust, which in turn can become a crucial opportunity structure for the success of populist political parties. The multilevel crises that both Greece and Turkey have faced in recent years have been facilitated by the increasing appeal of majoritarianism.

Keywords Democracy · Clientelism · Transparency
Social capital · Trust · Greece · Turkey · Polarization · Populism

The Case of Greece

The successful completion of the 1985–1986 constitutional amendment despite the heavy opposition that it raised comprised evidence for the emerging hegemonic role of PASOK in Greek politics towards the end of the twentieth century. PASOK and its leader Andreas Papandreou were able to set the blueprint of Greek politics for the following decades and define the operational framework of state performance. As the president was now limited to a largely ceremonial role and no institutional provisions aimed to promote the role of the judiciary, the Greek democratic regime took a clear majoritarian shift. The confrontational character of

© The Author(s) 2018   73
I.N. Grigoriadis, *Democratic Transition and the Rise of Populist
Majoritarianism*, Reform and Transition in the Mediterranean,
DOI 10.1007/978-3-319-57556-8_6

the 1986 amendment was not the exception. Populism repeatedly proved to be a successful political strategy, helping PASOK consolidate its political hegemony. As majoritarian politics were poised to instrumentalize and foster divisions in the name of "pure" popular sovereignty instead of healing them, Greek politics remained highly confrontational for several years after the controversial amendment. The concerns of many of the opponents of the constitutional reform package proved to be founded. These were not linked with any perceived immaturity of the people, but exactly with a possible conscious choice to promote institutional reform, which could make it more difficult to achieve cooperative and consensus-based solutions. As Aristovoulos Manessis, one of Greece's most prominent constitutional law experts at the time of the 1985 crisis put it:

> This distrust and the concomitant constant concern are not due to any perceived immaturity of the electoral body and the parliament. On the contrary, they are explained through the fear that the people, with its maturity, could wish to exploit the liberal and democratic constitutional frameworks to promote sociopolitical claims and institutional change.[1]

Manessis also pointed at how majoritarianism could threaten the core of the democratic regime:

> As the holders of the executive power, however, have at their disposal, by definition, the state apparatus -equipped today with the most sophisticated means to impose material and ideological coercion- it facilitates de facto the weakening or abolition of the principle of popular sovereignty. A democratic regime is under threat of abolition, if the reinforcement of the executive power is not combined with systematic provisions for enhanced guarantees in favour of individual and political freedom, the securing of functioning institutions that obstruct the abuse of power, for the more rational implementation of parliamentary control and the introduction of new instruments of popular control..[2]

Weakened checks and balances did not result in uncompromised popular sovereignty and "true democracy" but governmental or more accurately prime ministerial superpowers. The reinforcement of popular sovereignty ended up meaning the reinforcement of political parties and in the end of the Prime Minister. Excessive trust in the ability of political parties to regulate themselves and particularly in the ability of the government and the opposition to reach solutions without the existence of effective balancing mechanisms turned out to be not givens but *desiderata*.[3] In the end, what the amendment critics warned as the most likely outcome of the crisis turned out to be correct. A Prime-Minister-centred regime was the outcome of this process.[4] The Prime Minister became the key power broker, and his private office and advisors ended up usurping powers that normally belonged to the cabinet or the parliament. The Prime Minister acquired powers that led constitutional law experts to call the Greek Prime Minister "*sui generis* emperor" and "elected monarch".[5] As Manessis eloquently put in his book about the constitutional reform of 1986,

> The executive power remained disproportionately strong, as the only modification was the transfer of the real competences of the President of the Republic nominally to the parliament or the government, yet in practice personally to the prime minister, as an axis of a unified power centre. Against what could be called "prime ministerial state," there are no institutional checks and balances. Citizens reasonably mistrust any power actor, no matter how much democratic legitimation, direct or indirect, he may enjoy, which may have acquired, implied or usurped in multiple ways. [6]

Another critical side effect was the facilitation of the virtual subordination of the state to the government party priorities and objectives.[7] The constitutional reform of 1986 led to the substantial weakening of the institutional structures aiming to balance the power of the government. There was a virtual lack of effective checks and balances against the power of the Prime Minister, and this has been considered the source of many of the ills of the Greek political system. Clientelism and pork-barrel politics grew to unprecedented levels, while the appointment of party officials at all the levels of state bureaucracy resulted not only in complete control of the state by the government party but also a substantial decline in its performance and reform capacity.[8] The *esprit de corps* of Greek bureaucracy sharply declined. High levels of corruption, dwindling pluralism and transparency, nepotism, the decreasing quality and growing arrogance of political personnel have been named among the consequences.[9] Lack of tolerance for dissenting views dominated not only the political but also the academic realm. In the absence of a strong civil society that could potentially balance the power of the government and prevent the complete takeover of power by political parties, political leaders became untouchables. The parliament took advantage of constitutional immunity provisions, which gave government members virtual immunity for their deeds. All these contributed to an ever-lower quality of decision-making, which undermined Greece's institutional, social and economic outlook. The country avoided an earlier economic crisis, due to the positive effect of concomitant developments, such as EU funding, migration and the end of the Cold War. Yet this also meant that addressing the problems was becoming increasingly difficult.[10]

As problems could be concealed in global "fair weather" conditions, there was little concern about the negative effects of majoritarianism. The constitutional amendment of 2001 failed to address the pending issues and created additional problems.[11] Further institutional decline allowed the complete takeover of government policy by populist clientelistic considerations in the critical 2004–2009 Kostas Karamanlis[12] administration. Hence, Greece was institutionally weak and vulnerable to external shocks. When the global economic crisis hit Europe, Greece was among the least prepared states to cope with emerging challenges. The outbreak of the Greek crisis in 2009 reflected deeper problems and institutional shortcomings that the crisis only aggravated. It also reflected deep divisions and polarization in Greek society, which decades of majoritarian politics had intensified. Low social capital and the absence of strong civil society institutions meant that acute political party divisions would deter consensus-building and would lead to the toleration of a culture of anomy and violence. The Athens riots of December 2008 were a harbinger of the social and political decline that eventually led to the economic meltdown. Greece's formal bankruptcy in 2012 reached beyond the realm of economics. To that, the rising tide of populist majoritarianism was a key contributing factor. Pappas has underscored out how populism has pervaded the Greek political system since the 1970s[13] and has established that a dominant political paradigm has electorally punished any reformist attempts.[14] The meteoric rise of left-wing populist SYRIZA from electoral obscurity to nearly missing the absolute majority of seats in the Greek parliament in the January 2015 elections attested to the validity of Pappas' points.

The Impact of the Electoral Law

In their insightful study of Greek majoritarianism, Kovras and Loizides have pointed out at its deleterious effects regarding the outbreak and the prolongation of the Greek economic crisis.[15] While Greece was not alone among EU member states in facing a profound economic crisis in 2009, it became the only EU member state where big political parties failed to join forces in implementing a reform programme, what was implemented failed to deliver quick results and the country appeared to be in a vicious circle of recession. While the authors identified the electoral law among the reasons for Greece's poor crisis performance, it would be important to point that proportional representation was tested in Greece in 1989. The results were anything but satisfactory in terms of government performance. Greece had three parliamentary elections within less than a year, while two short-lived coalition governments failed to mitigate mounting polarization and avert a serious economic crisis.

In spring 1989, the PASOK government decided to amend the electoral law to a virtually proportional system, when it became clear that it could no more win the plurality of votes. The new law would obstruct a single-party government of its chief competitor which was now expected to win a plurality of votes. Predictably, New Democracy collected 44.3% of the vote in the 18 June 1989 elections, failing to form a single-party government. A coalition government of the centre-right New Democracy and the left "Coalition of the Left and the Progress" was established for some weeks only to secure the impeachment of the former Prime Minister Andreas Papandreou together with six former ministers and two high-ranking bureaucrats on corruption charges, which would otherwise lapse, due to a restrictive constitutional clause. The decision of the "Coalition of the Left and the Progress" to establish a coalition government with New Democracy even for a limited time and purpose was considered as "treason" by PASOK. This shed very negative connotations on the possibility of coalition governments. In the 5 November 1989 elections, New Democracy won 46.2% remaining again three seats away from parliamentary majority. A tripartite coalition government under the renowned economist Xenophon Zolotas was formed in order to address the serious economic crisis which had emerged and pave the ground for a third election. On 8 April 1950, New Democracy collected 46.8% of the vote and 150 seats, just the half of the 300 seats of the Greek parliament. Yet it could secure the support of two other deputies and establish a single-party government with a razor-thin majority. While New Democracy restored "enhanced proportional representation", its small majority proved critical in the inability of the government to put forward economic and political reforms. The resistance of clientelistic networks within the Greek public sector proved strong and averted the necessary economic reform. Eventually, the government lost the confidence of the parliament and fell in September 1993, because of its intention to find a compromise solution in Greece's name dispute with the Former Yugoslav Republic of Macedonia (FYROM). In the elections of 10 October 1993, PASOK won a comfortable parliamentary majority with 46.9% of the vote thanks to the restoration of "enhanced proportional system". While the latter did provide strong single-party governments that bred clientelism and patronage undermining the efficiency of the Greek public sector until the outbreak of the Greek economic crisis, the 1989–1990 experience pointed that proportional representation would be anything but a panacea for Greece's political woes.

The Populist Curse

Under these conditions, the constitutional reform proposals of the SYRIZA–ANEL coalition government that reflected these majoritarian views met with strong dissent. Even former supporters of such reforms such as Evangelos Venizelos, who had been a key figure in the 2001 constitutional amendment, expressing majoritarian preferences, accused the SYRIZA–ANEL government of 'undermining Greece's parliamentary democracy'. In particular, Tsipras' emphasis on referendums and the direct election of the president were the two most important proposals pointing at the reinforcement of majoritarianism. Nevertheless, the experience of the 6 July 2015 referendum that shook Greek politics by bringing the country to the brink of exit from the European Union and the Eurozone further polarized an already deeply divided Greek society, and produced a result which the Tsipras government itself failed to respect was a defining one. In fact, it pointed not only against the proliferation of referendums as a political instrument, but even against their use within the limits of the current constitution.

The polarized nature of Greek politics has been considered to be one of the key contributing factors to the failed response of the Greek political system to the multifold crisis that has hit the country since fall 2009. While other EU member states that faced similar challenges, such as Ireland, Portugal and Spain, could address the crisis through grand coalition governments that took unpopular but inevitable reform decisions and were able to reverse the economic decline, Greece was caught in a vicious circle of populist antireform rhetoric and unrealistic promises by leading opposition parties that minimized public tolerance towards unpopular reforms and facilitated their rise to power, but made a complete reversal on promises inevitable once in power. New Democracy under Antonis Samaras used this tactic while in opposition between 2009 and 2012. Fierce opposition to austerity policies disappeared when Samaras became Prime Minister of a coalition government in June 2012. This time it was SYRIZA's turn under Alexis Tsipras to engage in aggressive populist rhetoric. SYRIZA escalated its attacks against the coalition government arguing that the government were "traitors" to the Greek people and advanced the interests of Greece's creditors. SYRIZA came to power in a seemingly paradoxical coalition with the far-right "Independent Greeks" party (Anexartitoi Ellines-ANEL) following the election of 25 January 2015. Following a disastrous six-month negotiation with Greece's creditors which culminated with the imposition of capital controls, Prime Minister Tsipras signed in July 2015 a third memorandum agreement with even harsher austerity measures. While Tsipras was able to score a new electoral victory in the snap elections of 20 September 2015, these manoeuvres further undermined trust in Greek politics, as well as the implementation of reform and greatly complicated Greece's return to economic growth and political stability. Introducing a constitutional amendment debate was one of the instruments the coalition government used to lead the political debate.[16] This became more relevant, given the rising economic woes that led the SYRIZA-ANEL government to sign a fourth memorandum agreement in May 2017.

THE CASE OF TURKEY

Turkey's democratic consolidation took longer and became indexed to the country's membership application to the European Union, as well as the confrontation between the religious conservative Justice and Development Party (*Adalet ve Kalkınma Partisi-AKP*) and the secularist state elite. While the EU-powered reform zeal dissipated after 2005, the case for reinforcing the majoritarian elements of Turkey's democratic regime gained traction, as the AKP government was interested in eliminating the tutelary role of bureaucracy. The introduction by referendum in 2007 of the direct election of the president and the official endorsement by the AKP of a constitutional reform programme that would turn Turkey into a *sui generis* presidential democracy have put the question of majoritarianism into the heart of contemporary Turkish politics and have also highlighted its relevance. Populist strategies contributing to rising social and political polarization have raised concerns about a growing socio-political divide between the religious conservative and the secularist segments of Turkish society, between the Turkish majority and the Kurdish minority as well as about the takeover of the state apparatus by government party affiliates. A constitutional reform was seen as a remedy for existing institutional shortcomings: A new constitution was expected to provide the institutional structure for the resolution of long-standing political and social challenges. This would mean providing stronger and more efficient check-and-balance mechanisms, which would mitigate the threat for power accumulation, improve transparency and the rule of law. It would also mean the establishment of inclusive institutions that would embrace all different groups and maintain high levels of both social responsiveness and responsibility. Bridging the divides between Turks and Kurds, conservatives and secularists and providing a blueprint for a pluralistic society would be essential features of Turkey's new constitution.

Nevertheless, developments since the 12 September 2010 constitutional referendum have pointed towards the stark reinforcement of the majoritarian features of the state at the expense of the ability of institutions to address the fundamental challenges of the Turkish society. This majoritarian trend became stronger following the election of Recep Tayyip Erdoğan to the presidency, the double parliamentary elections of 2015 and the collapse of the Kurdish peace process. The introduction of a strong presidential system became the priority of the AKP administration, and all discussions about improving state performance through consensus-building, check-and-balance mechanisms and ensuring the pluralistic character of state institutions were shelved. The abortive military coup of 15 July 2016 was a painful reminder about the threats that Turkish democracy has faced from its military and a rare opportunity for forging national unity. Yet this opportunity was missed following the 20 July 2016 declaration of a state of emergency, the suspension of constitutional protection of key human rights and freedoms and the indiscriminate dismissals, detentions and arrests of dissidents. Consensus-building efforts were reversed, and the existence of multiple divides within the Turkish society beyond the conservative–secularist axis came to the fore.

In light of these developments, pursuing a constitutional reform aiming to underscore a majoritarian shift of the Turkish political system appeared in the view of the AKP government to be essential for the country to meet its formidable domestic and foreign policy challenges.

This was reflected in the constitutional amendment bill submitted on 10 December 2016. Nevertheless, this initiative met with the objection of leading constitutional law experts on two grounds. First, putting forward a constitutional amendment process before the expiration of the state of emergency meant that there could be no free and open public debate about the new constitution. In the views of Ibrahim Kaboğlu,[17] a prominent professor of constitutional law,

> How is the constitutional process to be taken forward under the state of emergency? How are we to obtain information about talks that are held behind closed doors? When will people be able to hold demonstrations in the street over the constitution without being truncheoned, kicked and given rough treatment by our police? The precondition for starting public debate over the constitution is the lifting of the state of emergency. For one thing, public debate over the constitution cannot be started until the state of emergency has been lifted. Secondly, constitutional amendment cannot be made until the state of emergency has been lifted. Thirdly, without lifting the state of emergency, constitutional amendment that will entail regime change most certainly cannot be made. ... The constitution to emerge may be a new constitution with its own date. But it will be the 15 July constitution and will be a constitution that falls short of the gains we have made.[18]

Second, apart from the timing of the constitutional amendment process, another key feature was the reinforcement of the executive against the legislative and judiciary. In the view of Prime Minister Binali Yıldırım, this was actually a positive step, as it would improve government performance:

> The parliament performing its law-making and review duties is being strengthened. Similarly is strengthened the presidency which will exercise its executive duty... Authority confusion is coming to an end, the presidency comes to the point of making every arrangement it deems necessary for its executive duties through its decrees; so is in a way the influence of the parliament on the executive and of the executive on the parliament reduced to the minimum. This reinforces both the parliament and the executive, but above all this introduced amendment brings an end to the era of coalitions. We begin a process which produces a stable strong government and together with that stability. I wish this future amendment be auspicious, lucky for our country, our nation.[19]

Most constitutional law experts did not agree with that judgement. What attracted their criticism was that the majoritarian features of the constitutional draft were stronger than ever, to the extent that they could potentially question the democratic nature of the constitution. The concentration of executive power in the hands of the president, the emphasis on strong and stable power, the weakening of the checks-and-balances role of the legislative and the judiciary raised concerns about the advancement of authoritarian tendencies and the decline of state performance.

In the view of Ergun Özbudun, professor of constitutional law, the claim of "legislative and executive organs being strengthened" was unfounded:

> "What we have here is the weakening of the legislative power while the president, with full executive powers, forms a parliament under his influence.[20]

Hikmet Sami Türk, a former member of the parliament and law professor, argued along more alarming lines:

> Supposedly, they are annulling martial law, but the president will be able to declare a state of emergency. All this power is a sign that Turkey will be under one-man rule. If the president has the power to appoint any minister, that means he will have the power to renew the parliament as well. If he has the power to structure the whole government, then there will be no control mechanisms whatsoever. ... If this proposal is approved, a Turkish-style, corrupt presidential system will be put into effect. The president will be able to rule with decrees and there will be no more laws. Democracy in Turkey will come to an end."[21]

Turk also raised the point that if the constitutional draft were approved, it will be nearly impossible to try the president, not only due to the qualified majorities involved in the impeachment process but also because the president as a political party leader will have a decisive influence on the deputies themselves.[22] Some experts came to the point of comparing the position of the president under the constitutional draft with that of the Sultan in the first Ottoman constitution of 1876.[23] Similar were the concerns raised in an opinion of the Venice Commission of the Council of Europe on the eve of the referendum.[24]

All these rather pessimistic accounts were not only linked to the adverse circumstances linked to the abortive coup of 15 July 2016 and the concomitant declaration of the state of emergency. It would be hard to imagine a free political debate about Turkey's constitutional future under the restrictive conditions of a state of emergency. Beyond that fact, what was highlighted was that reinforcing the majoritarian elements of the Turkish constitution, weakening the existing checks-and-balances mechanisms and introducing a strong presidential system in place of the existing parliamentary were not only undermining state performance in Turkey. It also posed a threat for the democratic nature of the regime. A constitutional amendment that would not contribute to the bridging of the divides between Turkey's conservatives, secularists and Kurdish nationalists but on the contrary to further polarization would not improve government performance. Resolving the Kurdish issue, achieving mutual respect for conservative and secular lifestyles and addressing the domestic and international security challenges would require not majoritarian but consensus-building initiatives. These appeared, however, to be in short supply in the text and during the debate of the constitutional draft. The approval of the proposed constitutional draft in the referendum of 16 April 2017 is likely to further aggravate the shortcomings of politics of populist majoritarianism in Turkey.

NOTES

1. Aristovoulos I. Manessis, "Η Νομικοπολιτική Θέση του Προέδρου της Δημοκρατίας κατά το Κυβερνητικό Σχέδιο Συντάγματος [The Juridicopolitical Status of the President of the Republic According to the Government Constitutional Draft]" in Aristovoulos I. Manessis, ed., Συνταγματική Θεωρία και Πράξη, Τόμος I [Constitutional Theory and Practice, Volume I] (Athens: Sakkoula [Σάκκουλα], 1980), p. 624, cited in Tassopoulos, Τα Θεσμικά Αντίβαρα της Εξουσίας και η Αναθεώρηση του Συντάγματος [Institutional Checks and Balances and Constitutional Amendment], p. 52.
2. Aristovoulos I. Manessis, Η Συνταγματική Αναθεώρηση του 1986: Μιά Κριτική Αποτίμηση της Νομικοπολιτικής Σημασίας της [The Constitutional Reform of 1986: A Critical Evaluation of its Juridicopolitical Significance] (Thessaloniki: Παρατηρητής [Paratiritis], 1989), pp. 145–146.
3. Alivizatos, Το Σύνταγμα και οι Εχθροί του στη Νεοελληνική Ιστορία 1800–2010 [The Constitution and its Enemies in Modern Greek History 1800–2010].

4. Dimitris Kaltsonis, *Ελληνική Συνταγματική Ιστορία, Τόμος Ι*: *1941–2001 [Greek Constitutional History, Volume II: 1941–2001]* (Athens: Ξιφαράς [Xifaras], 2010), pp. 156–59.

5. Antonis Makrydimitris, "Οι Αρμοδιότητες του Προέδρου [The Competences of the President]", *Το Βήμα [To Vima]*, 4/2/2001.

6. Manessis, *Η Συνταγματική Αναθεώρηση του 1986: Μιά Κριτική Αποτίμηση της Νομικοπολιτικής Σημασίας της [The Constitutional Reform of 1986: A Critical Evaluation of its Juridicopolitical Significance]*, pp. 144–145.

7. Yannis Voulgaris, *Η Ελλάδα από τη Μεταπολίτευση στην Παγκοσμιοποίηση [Greece from Transition to Globalization]* (Athens: Πόλις [Polis], 2008), pp. 154–156.

8. On this, see Kevin Featherstone and Dimitris Papadimitriou, *The Limits of Europeanization: Reform Capacity and Policy Conflict in Greece* (London: Palgrave, 2008).

9. Alivizatos, *Το Σύνταγμα και οι Εχθροί του στη Νεοελληνική Ιστορία 1800–2010 [The Constitution and its Enemies in Modern Greek History 1800–2010]*, pp. 538–539.

10. Ioannis N Grigoriadis, "Greek Tragedy", *World Policy Journal*, Vol. 28, no. 2 (2011), pp. 103–105.

11. For a succinct commentary, see Alivizatos and Eleftheriadis, "South European Briefing-the Greek Constitutional Amendments of 2001", pp. 70–71.

12. Kostas Karamanlis, Prime Minister of Greece between 2004 and 2009, is a nephew of the former President and Prime Minister Konstantinos Karamanlis.

13. Takis S. Pappas, "Populist Democracies: Post-Authoritarian Greece and Post-Communist Hungary", *Government and Opposition*, Vol. 49, no. 01 (2014b).

14. Takis S. Pappas, "Why Greece Failed", *Journal of Democracy*, Vol. 24, no. 2 (2013), pp. 42–44, Takis S. Pappas, *Populism and Crisis Politics in Greece* (London & New York: Palgrave Macmillan, 2014a), pp. 60–67.

15. Iosif Kovras and Neophytos Loizides, "The Greek Debt Crisis and Southern Europe: Majoritarian Pitfalls?", *Comparative Politics*, Vol. 47, no. 1 (2014), pp. 1–8.

16. Grigoriadis, *The Greece Constitutional Reform Process: Towards Direct Democracy and Secularism?*, pp. 1–2.

17. On 7 February 2017, Ibrahim Kaboğlu himself was sacked together with hundreds of other state university faculty members and civil servants by presidential decree for alleged "links to terrorist organizations". See Hümeyra Pamuk, Daren Butler and Nick Tattersall, *Turkey Sacks 4,400 More Civil Servants, Including Teachers and Police* (Reuters: Istanbul,

2017), available from http://www.reuters.com/article/us-turkey-security-dismissals-idUSKBN15N0KS [posted on 8/2/2017]. The crackdown on academia, which has been facilitated by the extended state of emergency has been one of the most alarming symptoms about the course of Turkish democracy.

18. Istanbul Office, "AKP and MHP Agree on the Constitutional Text-Experts Warn of a 15 July Constitution", *Cumhuriyet*, 14/12/2016.

19. Ankara Bürosu, *Başbakan Yıldırım'dan Anayasa Değişikliği Teklifi Açıklaması* (TRT Haber: Ankara, 2016), available from http://www.trthaber.com/haber/gundem/basbakan-yildirimdan-anayasa-degisikligi-teklifi-aciklamasi-287392.html [posted on 10/12/2016].

20. Hilal Köylü, "Law Experts Criticize Turkey's Proposed Constitutional Amendment", *Deutsche Welle*, 14/12/2016.

21. Ibid.

22. Ibid.

23. Ahmet Erdi Öztürk and İştar Gözaydın, "Turkey's Draft Constitutional Amendments: Harking Back to 1876?", *OpenDemocracy*, 20/12/2016.

24. European Commission for Democracy through Law (Venice Commission), *Turkey: Opinion on the Amendments to the Constitution Adopted by the Grand National Assembly on 21 January 2017 and to be Submitted to a National Referendum on 16 April 2017 [Opinion No. 875/2017]* (Strasbourg: Council of Europe, 2017)

REFERENCES

Nicos Alivizatos and Pavlos Eleftheriadis, "South European Briefing-the Greek Constitutional Amendments of 2001", *South European Society and Politics*, Vol. 7, no. 1 (2002), pp. 63–71.

Nicos C. Alivizatos, *Το Σύνταγμα και οι Εχθροί του στη Νεοελληνική Ιστορία 1800-2010 [The Constitution and its Enemies in Modern Greek History 1800–2010]* (Athens: Πόλις [Polis], 2011).

Ankara Bürosu, *Başbakan Yıldırım'dan Anayasa Değişikliği Teklifi Açıklaması* (TRT Haber: Ankara, 2016), available from http://www.trthaber.com/haber/gundem/basbakan-yildirimdan-anayasa-degisikligi-teklifi-aciklamasi-287392.html [posted on 10/12/2016].

European Commission for Democracy through Law (Venice Commission), *Turkey: Opinion on the Amendments to the Constitution Adopted by the Grand National Assembly on 21 January 2017 and to be Submitted to a National Referendum on 16 April 2017 [Opinion No. 875/2017]* (Strasbourg: Council of Europe, 2017).

Kevin Featherstone and Dimitris Papadimitriou, *The Limits of Europeanization: Reform Capacity and Policy Conflict in Greece* (London: Palgrave, 2008).

Ioannis N Grigoriadis, "Greek Tragedy", *World Policy Journal*, Vol. 28, no. 2 (2011), pp. 101–109.

Ioannis N. Grigoriadis, *The Greece Constitutional Reform Process: Towards Direct Democracy and Secularism?* (International Institute for Democracy & Electoral Assistance (IDEA): Stockholm, 2016), available from http://www.constitutionnet.org/news/greece-constitutional-reform-process-towards-direct-democracy-and-secularism [posted on 24/8/2016].

Dimitris Kaltsonis, *Ελληνική Συνταγματική Ιστορία, Τόμος Ι₁: 1941–2001 [Greek Constitutional History, Volume II: 1941–2001]* (Athens: Ξιφαράς [Xifaras], 2010).

Iosif Kovras and Neophytos Loizides, "The Greek Debt Crisis and Southern Europe: Majoritarian Pitfalls?", *Comparative Politics*, Vol. 47, no. 1 (2014), pp. 1–20.

Istanbul Office, "AKP and MHP Agree on the Constitutional Text-Experts Warn of a 15 July Constitution", *Cumhuriyet*, 14/12/2016.

Hilal Köylü, "Law Experts Criticize Turkey's Proposed Constitutional Amendment", *Deutsche Welle*, 14/12/2016.

Antonis Makrydimitris, "Οι Αρμοδιότητες του Προέδρου [The Competences of the President]", *Το Βήμα [To Vima]*, 4/2/2001.

Aristovoulos I. Manessis, "Η Νομικοπολιτική Θέση του Προέδρου της Δημοκρατίας κατά το Κυβερνητικό Σχέδιο Συντάγματος [The Juridicopolitical Status of the President of the Republic According to the Government Constitutional Draft]" in Aristovoulos I. Manessis, ed., *Συνταγματική Θεωρία και Πράξη, Τόμος Ι [Constitutional Theory and Practice, Volume I]* (Athens: Sakkoula [Σάκκουλα], 1980).

Aristovoulos I. Manessis, *Η Συνταγματική Αναθεώρηση του 1986: Μιά Κριτική Αποτίμηση της Νομικοπολιτικής Σημασίας της [The Constitutional Reform of 1986: A Critical Evaluation of its Juridicopolitical Significance]* (Thessaloniki: Παρατηρητής [Paratiritis], 1989).

Hümeyra Pamuk, Daren Butler and Nick Tattersall, *Turkey Sacks 4,400 More Civil Servants, Including Teachers and Police* (Reuters: Istanbul, 2017), available from http://www.reuters.com/article/us-turkey-security-dismissals-idUSKBN15N0KS [posted on 8/2/2017].

Ahmet Erdi Öztürk and İştar Gözaydın, "Turkey's Draft Constitutional Amendments: Harking Back to 1876?", *OpenDemocracy*, 20/12/2016.

Takis S. Pappas, "Why Greece Failed", *Journal of Democracy*, Vol. 24, no. 2 (2013), pp. 31–45.

Takis S. Pappas, *Populism and Crisis Politics in Greece* (London & New York: Palgrave Macmillan, 2014a).

Takis S. Pappas, "Populist Democracies: Post-Authoritarian Greece and Post-Communist Hungary", *Government and Opposition*, Vol. 49, no. 01 (2014b), pp. 1–23.

Yannis A. Tassopoulos, *Τα Θεσμικά Αντίβαρα της Εξουσίας και η Αναθεώρηση του Συντάγματος [Institutional Checks and Balances and Constitutional Amendment]* (Athens & Thessaloniki: Σάκκουλα [Sakkoula], 2007).

Yannis Voulgaris, *Η Ελλάδα από τη Μεταπολίτευση στην Παγκοσμιοποίηση [Greece from Transition to Globalization]* (Athens: Πόλις [Polis], 2008).

CHAPTER 7

Conclusion

Abstract In both Greece and Turkey, the rise of populist majoritarianism was linked to the completion of the democratic consolidation process. Nevertheless, it has contributed to the exacerbation of existing social and political divisions and undermined the integrity and efficiency of democratic institutions. As both countries face formidable challenges, "Grexit" in the case of Greece and a shift to competitive authoritarianism in the case of Turkey, introducing institutions and constitutional documents aiming to build consensus and trust is an imperative task.

Keywords Grexit · Greece · Turkey · Majoritarianism · Competitive authoritarianism · Consensus · Mild democracy

REVISITING MAJORITARIANISM IN GREECE AND TURKEY

The comparative study of Greek and Turkish encounters with the rising tide of populist majoritarianism confirms that the main conclusions of the works of Lijphart maintain their relevance.[1] Moreover, it instructs that majoritarianism can serve as a crucial tool for populist parties—left or right-wing—that wish to establish a political hegemony by capitalizing on pre-existing social divisions. The manipulation of the latter has proven a shrewd political strategy, as far as the electoral fortunes of these parties are concerned. On the other hand, populist majoritarianism has left deep social wounds and prevented the cultivation of social consensus.

© The Author(s) 2018
I.N. Grigoriadis, *Democratic Transition and the Rise of Populist Majoritarianism*, Reform and Transition in the Mediterranean, DOI 10.1007/978-3-319-57556-8_7

Low social trust is fed by politics of majoritarianism, and vice versa, in what becomes a self-fulfilling prophecy of electoral success and a vicious circle of institutional underperformance.

Majoritarianism is not intrinsically linked with presidentialism or parliamentarism; it can have different faces in different political contexts. While in Greece majoritarianism was expressed in terms of virtually cancelling the balancing role of the president and introducing a "prime ministerial state", in Turkey it followed the path of reinforcing the powers of the president, up to the point of a government system that could qualify as Latin American "*decretismo*". In cases of transition states where levels of social capital are low and institutional performance leaves much to be desired, the concomitant corrosion of checks and balances that such majoritarian steps bring about can lead to increasing polarization and state inefficiency, and eventually contribute to a slowdown or even reversal of the democratic consolidation process.

Greece

The study of the Greek case since the 1980s shows us that the dominance of populist majoritarianism could help deepen divisions, stifle pluralism, contribute to the subordination of state bureaucracy to party clientelistic networks, reduce institutional performance, diminish the quality of political institutions and personnel, foster corruption and deepen social divisions.[2] Decreasing levels of transparency, rising levels of corruption and a sharp decline of social capital could also be observed, while political participation was reaching historic lows.[3] While the shift of the Greek democracy towards populist majoritarianism does not comprise the single reason for these developments, it appears to be one of the leading contributing factors. The dilution of existing checks and balances, the fragmentation of Greek society and the disintegration of state bureaucracy have been among the key underlying factors for the profound economic and social crisis that has befallen upon Greece since 2009. An intrinsic feature is also the high degree of social polarization, which has found expression in several violent incidents, not least of which is the Athens riots of December 2008. While the Greek economic crisis has not threatened the viability of Greek democracy, the meteoric rise of antidemocratic political parties, such as the neo-Nazi "Golden Dawn", is an alarming symptom of the degeneration of the democratic regime due to the collapse of trust to political parties and

Fig. 7.1 Pro-EU, anti-government demonstration on 15 June 2016 in Athens' Syntagma Square

other democratic institutions. Moreover, the use of populist discourse by SYRIZA during its swift rise to power but also by other parties such as SYRIZA's junior coalition government partner, the far-right ANEL and the neo-Nazi "Golden Dawn" also pointed to a crucial feature of politics of populist majoritarianism. Describing the supporters of the reform programme introduced by Greece's creditors as "traitors", questioning their loyalty to Greece or even employing vocabulary normally applied to Quislings or Greek collaborators of the Nazi occupation forces during 1941–1944 may have contributed to the consolidation of the SYRIZA voter base and improved its electoral prospects. On the other hand, it undermined any efforts of dialogue and consensus-building across the political spectrum, which also hit SYRIZA back as a boomerang when it came to power in January 2015 and attempted to implement the reform programme it had long chastised (Fig. 7.1).[4]

The discussion on Greece's rising majoritarian tendencies does not imply that the SYRIZA–ANEL constitutional reform proposals are likely to be adopted. Considering the declining fortunes of the coalition government, the constitutional amendment proposals are not likely to be realized. Opposition parties whose endorsement is essential to meet the qualified majority necessary for the success of the process have declared their intentions to vote against the government proposals or submit their own. Yet this does not mean that a reform of the Greek constitution is not due. A short volume which a group of constitutional law experts and businesspersons published suggesting a "new constitution" for Greece could be a useful starting point for discussion. Among other steps, and in accordance to the SYRIZA-ANEL government proposal it suggested the introduction of the constructive vote of no-confidence in order to strengthen government stability. On the other hand, contrary to the government proposals, it envisioned the reinforcement of the competences of the president as a checks-and-balances mechanism against the powers of the prime minister, but maintained and made easier his indirect election. To combat corruption, it suggested the election of members of parliament through fixed party ballot lists and not through giving voters the right to choose their preferred candidate. It also suggested the facilitation of lifting the immunities of ministers and members of parliament, so they could face justice when prosecuted.[5]

Turkey

In the case of Turkey, the rising tide of populist majoritarianism was linked with the end of the tutelary role of the civil and military bureaucracy and the consolidation of the hegemonic position of the AKP. Yet the abolition of the tutelary role of the judiciary and the military was a necessary but not sufficient condition for the consolidation of Turkish democracy. If the elimination of non-democratic checks and balances were an indispensable part of democratic consolidation, so is the care about avoiding majoritarian extremes and forging a balance between different democratically legitimate state institutions. The removal of these antidemocratic checks and balances could reduce regime performance and create other threats to democracy, if not matched with legal measures aiming to foster a system of democratic control. The establishment of a strong and effective system of checks and balances does not reduce the performance of government. It may take more time for decisions to be made, but these decisions are more likely to be inclusive and sound. Moreover, such a system would make corruption more difficult and remains a key guardian against the degeneration of the regime into veiled authoritarianism . Manessis aptly described the threat that the tyranny of the majority comprised to democracy as follows:

> ...The variability of majority and minority is an element of democracy...What is crucial in a democratic regime is the securing of political

and ideological freedom and pluralism, the securing, namely, of the will of the majority as well as the ability of the minority to become majority. Therefore, the protection of the given minority, so that it is not at the mercy of the majority, which could potentially turn out to be a merciless one. And this not out of concern to favour the opposition and the minorities, but to safeguard that all the governed enjoy the possibility to express different views, approach critically and challenge in practice power institutions in the framework of the "political game" without any unpleasant consequences to them. ....freedom, which is worth something and has practical importance, is not the freedom of those agreeing but the freedom of those disagreeing.... Freedom is always, at least, the freedom of the person thinking differently.[6]

The points raised in this study help us better understand the nature of the current constitutional reform in Turkey. Failing to reinforce democratic checks and balances following the end of the tutelary role of the military, the judiciary and administration has led to a risk of further power accumulation in the hands of the executive. Populism-driven polarizing tactics which have been intensively employed by the AKP since the June 2015 elections may have proved rather fruitful in electoral terms but have deepened already existing divides between ethnic Turks and Kurds, religious conservatives and secularists, as well as within the religious conservatives.

The abortive coup of 15 July 2016 which could have become a symbol of national unity and democratic regeneration ended up in further fragmenting the society, due to the extensive anti-dissident purges that were held under the auspices of the state of emergency. Under these extraordinary circumstances, populism-driven majoritarianism proved a crucial opportunity structure for President Erdoğan and the AKP administration in their effort to have their preferred constitution ratified via referendum.

As majoritarianism has had deep roots in Turkish constitutional history and practice, it has been relatively uncommon to argue in favour of developing consensus-based institutions and limit the risk that power accumulation could pose to Turkey's democratic consolidation. On the other hand, the need to establish effective checks and balances that limit the power of the executive has become clearer, a *sine qua non* for the successful consolidation of Turkish democracy. Turkey's democratic consolidation could be better served through the introduction of a new liberal democratic constitution that would shed off the authoritarian vestiges of the 1982 Constitution and substitute liberal democratic checks and balances for the tutelary functions of the military, the judiciary and the administration.[7] In light of the above, the affirmative vote of the Turkish people in the constitutional referendum of 16 April 2017 is unlikely to bring Turkey closer to its democratic consolidation.

THE SPECTRE OF "GREXIT" IN GREECE

Following three memorandum agreements and a GDP drop of than 40% between 2009 and 2016, Greece's economic recovery remained elusive in early 2017. The failure of the SYRIZA–ANEL government to fulfil the unrealistic promises it gave in order to win the January 2015 elections disappointed its voters, while the government's unwillingness to wholeheartedly implement a genuine reform programme led to a vicious circle of economic recession and failure to meet the set fiscal targets. Cornered by its decision to endorse fiscal austerity measures but unable to exit recession, the government repeatedly resorted to populist rhetoric and polarization in the policy areas not directly affected by the memorandum agreement. Education, media and information, even the amendment of the constitution, became focal points of policy initiatives aiming to shift attention from the harsh economic reality and galvanize the government party voters, despite their disillusionment regarding economic policies.

The government's unwillingness to implement agreed measures, meet set economic targets and help the Greek economy stand to its feet again stoked fears about a relapse of a "Grexit" crisis, in case Greece's creditors appeared unwilling to agree to further refinancing Greece's debt. The prospect of Greece's withdrawal from the Eurozone and probably from the European Union itself lurked, as the government pondered between early elections and a new game of brinkmanship, with Greece's creditors under more adverse conditions than in summer 2015. Despite nine years of depression, Greece's economic and political future remained uncertain, with populist majoritarian tactics remaining intact.

THE SPECTRE OF COMPETITIVE AUTHORITARIANISM IN TURKEY

Meanwhile, fears about a "downturn in Turkish democracy"[8] and concerns about Turkey's drift towards a competitive authoritarian regime gained ground following the abortive coup of 15 July 2016 and the concomitant declaration of state of emergency. A sharp decline in human rights protection was noted by international human rights organizations. According to a Freedom House report, Turkey suffered the largest decline in freedoms among 195 countries during 2016. Its aggregate score declined by fifteen points from 53 to 38 (with 100 being the most free), while it maintained its "partly free" status in its record of freedoms together with 59 other countries.[9] The arrests of thousands of suspected coup plotters and dissidents, including leaders and members of the parliament of the pro-Kurdish Peoples' Democratic Party (Halkların Demokratik Partisi-HDP) facilitated under the state of emergency provisions, eliminated the space for any meaningful political debate. Reinvigorating the divisions within Turkish society boosted the fortunes of populist majoritarianism. The decision of the government to put forward the constitutional amendment process under the post-coup attempt conditions was an additional indication in the same direction. The introduction of a strong presidential system with weakened check-and-balance mechanisms along the lines described by Kalaycıoğlu[10] clearly pointed that majoritarianism was bound to thrive once again. As the constitutional draft was approved with 51.4 percent in the referendum of 16 April 2017, President Erdoğan and the AKP government won the desired popular endorsement of their shift towards majoritarianism. On the other hand, the thin margin of the victory, which occurred under state of emergency conditions, pointed at a deeply fragmented society whose divisions were unlikely to heal through populist majoritarian practices.

WHAT A "MILD DEMOCRACY" WOULD ENTAIL

What also becomes clear from the study of constitutional reform in Greece and Turkey is the difficulties emanating from the absence of a strong consensual and participant political culture for the successful function of a consensus democracy.[11] Existing social divisions can become useful instruments in the hands of populist parties of the left or the right in their aim to establish their political hegemony at the expense of dispensing any chance for the development of social capital. Lijphart's conclusion that "a consensus-oriented culture often provides the basis for and connections between the institutions of consensus democracy" is corroborated with this study (Lijphart 1999: 306).[12] Constitutional and institutional reforms aiming at reinforcing checks-and-balances mechanisms and cultivating a culture of social consensus remain of fundamental importance in countries characterized by low levels of social capital. Such reforms may include but are definitely not limited to electoral law reform and the introduction of proportional representation. Building up a "mild democracy" requires maturity of institutions, an efficient system of checks and balances, horizontal accountability, and establishment and operation of control mechanisms. This would lead to the shift from a "zero sum" to a "positive sum game" approach in the resolution of domestic political disputes and facilitate cross-party collaboration and alliances. Building consensus and trust in societies torn by ethnic, religious and ideological divides is not a luxury but a permissive condition for institutional performance catalysing democratic consolidation and economic prosperity. The recent experiences of Greece and Turkey provide ample evidence and can be highly instructive about the perils of ignoring this.

NOTES

1. Lijphart, *Patterns of Democracy: Government Forms and Performance in Thirty-Six Countries*, pp. 275–300, Lijphart, *Thinking About Democracy: Power Sharing and Majority Rule in Theory and Practice*, pp. 89–107.
2. Alivizatos, *Το Σύνταγμα και οι Εχθροί του στη Νεοελληνική Ιστορία 1800–2010 [The Constitution and its Enemies in Modern Greek History 1800–2010]*, pp. 666–667.
3. The abstention rate in the January 2015 elections reached 36.4 and in the September 2015 elections 44%. See Anastassios Adamopoulos, *Voter Turnout in Greek Elections Drops to New Historic Low: Infographic* (Greek Reporter: Athens, 2015), available from http://greece.greekreporter.com/2015/09/21/voter-turnout-in-greek-elections-drops-to-new-historic-low-infographic/#sthash.zGIbRnb3.dpuf.
4. For a succinct study of SYRIZA populism, see Cas Mudde, *SYRIZA: The Failure of the Populist Promise* (Cham, Switzerland: Palgrave Pivot, 2016), pp. 7–24.
5. Nicos C. Alivizatos et al., *Ένα Καινοτόμο Σύνταγμα για την Ελλάδα: Κείμενα Εργασίας [An Innovative Constitution for Greece: Working Papers]* (Athens: Μεταίχμιο [Metaechmio], 2016).
6. Manessis, *Η Συνταγματική Αναθεώρηση του 1986: Μιά Κριτική Αποτίμηση της Νομικοπολιτικής Σημασίας της [The Constitutional Reform of 1986: A Critical Evaluation of its Juridicopolitical Significance]*, pp. 126–128, Rosa Luxemburg, *Oeuvres II* (Paris: Maspero, 1969), pp. 82–83.
7. The draft prepared at the request of the Erdoğan government in 2007 by an experts committee led by Ergun Özbudun is a useful point of reference.

8. Meltem Müftüler-Baç and E. Fuat Keyman, "Turkey's Unconsolidated Democracy: The Nexus between Democratisation and Majoritarianism in Turkey" in Senem Aydın-Düzgit, Daniela Huber, Meltem Müftüler-Baç, E. Fuat Keyman, et al., eds., *Global Turkey in Europe III: Democracy, Trade, and the Kurdish Question in Turkey-EU Relations* (Rome: IAI & Edizioni Nuova Cultura, 2015), pp. 123–125.
9. Freedom House, *Freedom in the World 2017* (Washington DC: Freedom House, 2017), pp. 8, 12, 20.
10. Ersin Kalaycıoğlu, "The Challenge of à la Turca Presidentialism in Turkey" in Senem Aydın-Düzgit, Daniela Huber, Meltem Müftüler-Baç, E. Fuat Keyman, et al., eds., *Global Turkey in Europe III: Democracy, Trade, and the Kurdish Question in Turkey-EU Relations* (Rome: IAI & Edizioni Nuova Cultura, 2015), pp. 108–112.
11. Levent Gönenç, "Türkiye'de Hükümet Sistemi Değişikliği Tartışmaları: Olanaklar ve Olasılıklar Üzerine Bir Çalışma Notu" in Teoman Ergül, ed., *Başkanlık Sistemi* (Ankara: Türkiye Barolar Birliği, 2005), p. 11.
12. Lijphart, *Patterns of Democracy: Government Forms and Performance in Thirty-Six Countries*, p. 306.

REFERENCES

Anastassios Adamopoulos, *Voter Turnout in Greek Elections Drops to New Historic Low: Infographic* (Greek Reporter: Athens, 2015), available from http://greece.greekreporter.com/2015/09/21/voter-turnout-in-greek-elections-drops-to-new-historic-low-infographic/#sthash.zGIbRnb3.dpuf.

Nicos C. Alivizatos, *Το Σύνταγμα και οι Εχθροί του στη Νεοελληνική Ιστορία 1800–2010 [The Constitution and its Enemies in Modern Greek History 1800–2010]* (Athens: Πόλις [Polis], 2011).

Nicos C. Alivizatos, Panagis Vourloumis, Georgios Gerapetritis, Yannis Ktistakis, Stefanos Manos and Philippos Spyropoulos, *Ένα Καινοτόμο Σύνταγμα Για Την Ελλάδα: Κείμενα Εργασίας [an Innovative Constitution for Greece: Working Papers]* (Athens: Μεταίχμιο [Metaechmio], 2016).

Freedom House, *Freedom in the World 2017* (Washington DC: Freedom House, 2017).

Levent Gönenç, "Türkiye'de Hükümet Sistemi Değişikliği Tartışmaları: Olanaklar ve Olasılıklar Üzerine Bir Çalışma Notu" in Teoman Ergül, ed., *Başkanlık Sistemi* (Ankara: Türkiye Barolar Birliği, 2005), pp. 1–12.

Ersin Kalaycıoğlu, "The Challenge of à la Turca Presidentialism in Turkey" in Senem Aydın-Düzgit, Daniela Huber, Meltem Müftüler-Baç, E. Fuat Keyman, Michael Schwarz and Nathalie Tocci, eds., *Global Turkey in Europe III: Democracy, Trade, and the Kurdish Question in Turkey-EU Relations* (Rome: IAI & Edizioni Nuova Cultura, 2015), pp. 107–114.

Arend Lijphart, *Patterns of Democracy: Government Forms and Performance in Thirty-Six Countries* (New Haven, CT: Yale University Press, 1999).

Arend Lijphart, *Thinking About Democracy: Power Sharing and Majority Rule in Theory and Practice* (London & New York: Routledge, 2007).

Rosa Luxemburg, *Oeuvres II* (Paris: Maspero, 1969).

Aristovoulos I. Manessis, *Η Συνταγματική Αναθεώρηση του 1986: Μιά Κριτική Αποτίμηση της Νομικοπολιτικής Σημασίας της* [*The Constitutional Reform of 1986: A Critical Evaluation of its Juridicopolitical Significance*] (Thessaloniki: Παρατηρητής [Paratiritis], 1989).

Cas Mudde, *SYRIZA: The Failure of the Populist Promise* (Cham, Switzerland: Palgrave Pivot, 2016).

Meltem Müftüler-Baç and E. Fuat Keyman, "Turkey's Unconsolidated Democracy: The Nexus between Democratisation and Majoritarianism in Turkey" in Senem Aydın-Düzgit, Daniela Huber, Meltem Müftüler-Baç, E. Fuat Keyman, Michael Schwarz and Nathalie Tocci, eds., *Global Turkey in Europe III: Democracy, Trade, and the Kurdish Question in Turkey-EU Relations* (Rome: IAI & Edizioni Nuova Cultura, 2015), pp. 121–130.

Appendix I

Greek Constitutional Texts

A translation of the current text of the Greek constitution can be accessed at Hellenic Parliament, *The Constitution of Greece* (Hellenic Parliament: Athens, 2007), available from http://bit.ly/greekconstitution. (last accessed on 11 August 2017).

© The Editor(s) (if applicable) and The Author(s) 2018   99
I.N. Grigoriadis, *Democratic Transition and the Rise of Populist Majoritarianism*, Reform and Transition in the Mediterranean, DOI 10.1007/978-3-319-57556-8

Appendix II

Turkish Constitutional Texts

A translation of the current text of the Turkish constitution can be accessed at Turkish Grand National Assembly, *The Constitution of the Republic of Turkey* (Turkish Grand National Assembly: Ankara, 2017), available from http://bit.ly/turkishconstitution (last accessed on 11 August 2017).

© The Editor(s) (if applicable) and The Author(s) 2018   101
I.N. Grigoriadis, *Democratic Transition and the Rise of Populist Majoritarianism*, Reform and Transition in the Mediterranean, DOI 10.1007/978-3-319-57556-8

Index

© The Editor(s) (if applicable) and The Author(s) 2018
I.N. Grigoriadis, *Democratic Transition and the Rise of Populist Majoritarianism*, Reform and Transition in the Mediterranean, DOI 10.1007/978-3-319-57556-8

Printed in the United States
By Bookmasters